TREATING THE "UNTREATABLE"

TREATING THE "UNTREATABLE"

HEALING IN THE REALMS OF MADNESS

Ira Steinman

KARNAC

First published in 2009 by
Karnac Books Ltd
118 Finchley Road
London NW3 5HT

British Library Cataloguing in Publication Data

A.C.I.P. for this book is available from the British Library

ISBN-13: 978-1-85575-680-9 (UK edition)
ISBN-13: 978-1-85575-609-0 (US Edition)

Edited, designed, and produced by Sheffield Typesetting
www.sheffieldtypesetting.com
e-mail: admin@sheffieldtypesetting.com

www.karnacbooks.com

CONTENTS

ABOUT THE AUTHOR   xi

PREFACE   xiii

CHAPTER ONE
Delusional reality   1

CHAPTER TWO
The psychotherapy of delusional states   7

CHAPTER THREE
Causes of a delusional orientation   15

CHAPTER FOUR
The method   19

CHAPTER FIVE
The history of the psychotherapy of schizophrenia
and delusional states   21

CHAPTER SIX
Psychotherapeutic technique and stages in the
psychotherapy of delusional states   29

APOLOGIA AND CLINICAL PRESENTATION   35

CHAPTER SEVEN
The Good Angel, the Bad Devil, the Smiling Man's Voice
and Mother-God   37

CHAPTER EIGHT
The pugilist, Mary, and the mother with the fiery halo   53

CHAPTER NINE
Two rats and the extraterrestrial   61

CHAPTER TEN
The ghost in the history   67

CHAPTER ELEVEN
Stalemate   73

CHAPTER TWELVE
Maya, Little, and the world of illusion   79

CHAPTER THIRTEEN
Death, Egyptian style   89

CHAPTER FOURTEEN
Nobody   93

CHAPTER FIFTEEN
The voice didn't win   103

CHAPTER SIXTEEN
The world class artist of the symbolic world: the Mafia,
the movie stars and the "Unconscious God"   115

CHAPTER SEVENTEEN
Can anyone that evil ever really die?   145

CHAPTER EIGHTEEN
The cheerleader   179

CHAPTER NINETEEN
Thoughts, lessons and conclusions   183

APPENDIX 1
Long-term studies on schizophrenia   191
    Brian Koehler, PhD

APPENDIX 2
Brief review of psychoanalytic perspectives on schizophrenia   199
    Brian Koehler, PhD

REFERENCES   203

In memory of my mother and father,
I dedicate this book to all
who joined me on life's
transforming
journey

Ira Steinman has focused on schizophrenia for 45 years; his early training ranged from studying with R. D. Laing to working at the National Academy of Sciences' Drug Efficacy Study, which evaluated all the antipsychotic medications available at that time. For more than 35 years, he has pursued an out-patient psychiatric practice in San Francisco where he has been able to demonstrate that an intensive psychoanalytic psychotherapy, in conjunction with the judicious use of antipsychotic medication, can help even the most lost and disturbed schizophrenic and delusional patients recover, heal and, at times, achieve a cure. With such an approach, some allegedly "untreatable" schizophrenics have been able to work their way off of antipsychotic medication and develop a satisfying life of relationships and function.

From the beginning of my psychiatric training more than forty years ago, I have been fascinated by people with delusional and schizophrenic disorders. Having treated quite a number of delusional patients from many different diagnostic categories over the intervening years, I'd like to present a theory and clinical examples of successful psychodynamic treatment of even the most disturbed and psychotic patients.

Since this is a problem that affects not only the schizophrenic or delusional patient but family and friends as well, I have written this book for the general public as well as interested members of the psychiatric profession, in the hope that more people will realise that there is much that can be done for such seemingly lost and confused people.

Many severely disturbed patients, diagnosed as schizophrenic or delusional, respond to antipsychotic medication, full-time or partial hospitalisation and reality-oriented, supportive psychotherapy. However, some of these confused people do not benefit from this supportive approach (primarily medication and cognitive therapy), remaining mired in a chaotic and deteriorating condition which leaves little hope for them or their families; they are considered hopeless and "untreatable".

Here are some facts about schizophrenia in the United States. The average prevalence rate is 3.4 per 1,000 people. One-year prevalence in adults aged 18 to 54 is estimated to be 1.3%. Each year, 100,000 people are newly diagnosed as schizophrenic. On any given day, 600,000 people are in active treatment for schizophrenia; well over two million people suffer from schizophrenia. Including family and friends, perhaps 10 million people in the US have a personal interest in the treatment of schizophrenia and delusional disorders.

Pharmaceutical companies, too, have an interest in the treatment of schizophrenia and delusional states. Through relentless advertising of antipsychotic medications and funding of groups oriented towards supportive care with antipsychotic medication, even medicines with tremendous potential for destructive glucose and lipid metabolism side effects have become the standard of care. When their children become schizophrenic or delusional, devoted families believe they have nowhere to turn but to a primarily drug-oriented approach which frequently blunts the symptoms but may do little to change the underlying thought processes and return their child to a more functional and related life.

If antipsychotic medication works, so much the better. All too often, however, antipsychotic medication merely covers over the disturbed and confused thinking that underlies such severe conditions. Gradually, patients may go through a revolving door of psychiatric hospitalisation, drug treatment, day hospitals and halfway houses. Some continue to deteriorate in spite of these efforts and become "untreatable" in the eyes of most mental health practitioners and psychiatrists. The best that is hoped for is an adjustment to reality, not a working through of underlying psychological issues and emotions which have been warded off.

I have found over the last 40 years of psychiatric practice, however, that a number of these allegedly "unresponsive" and "untreatable" severely disturbed patients, diagnosed as suffering from schizophrenia, paranoid delusional disorder and multiple personality disorder, have responded to an in-depth exploratory psychodynamic psychotherapy. In a number of cases, antipsychotic medication has been titrated down and stopped, as patients who had been floridly psychotic for decades began to understand not only the psychological factors leading to their deterioration, but the symbolic meaning to them of both delusions and hallucinations. With comprehension of the psychological underpinnings of their condition, delusions and hallucinations have diminished and ceased, and they have returned to a life of relationships and function.

Because this type of in-depth work with psychotic people is so rarely done, so frequently questioned, and so rarely written about, I have written *Treating the "Untreatable"*, a chronicle of twelve schizophrenic or delusional patients who responded to such a psychodynamic approach when all else had failed. Some of these patients had been hospitalised and medicated for years; others were in and out of hospitals repeatedly before an attempt was made to help them understand the meaning of their hallucinations, delusions and previously incomprehensible mental states.

My goal in writing this book is to demonstrate through these successful clinical examples that an intensive psychotherapy may aid even the most distressed through the morass of psychosis, where previous hospitalisations, courses of antipsychotic medication and ancillary treatments had been of little help. *Treating the "Untreatable"* articulates a rationale for the use of an intensive psychodynamic psychotherapy in such a disturbed population and proves false the current belief that such an in-depth exploratory psychotherapy is of no benefit in such severely disorganised patients.

Delusional people have their own belief systems; for them, consensually validated reality does not apply. They are in a world of their own, certain of the correctness of their perceptions and unresponsive to the supportive ministrations of friends and families. We have all seen them muttering to themselves and, even worse, responding. They seem beyond the ken of human discourse; there is no there, there.

The torment of the deluded is difficult for any of us to fathom. We brush past the shouting, gesticulating homeless "madman" on the street. We wonder why she sits quietly talking to herself for hours, oblivious to the day's events. We try to follow the convoluted thinking of the paranoid, or extend ourselves to listen to his fears and improbable anxieties. We see families giving up on loved ones who now seem beyond help and redemption. We see lives shattered by delusions and schizophrenic thought; more probably, we avert our eyes.

Once delusional, people are often beyond the pale for most of us. What they utter appears to be nonsensical. The paranoid terrors and grandiose schemes have little or no realistic basis. The inflated or deflated sense of self bears no relationship to other people's perceptions. If antipsychotic medication and social rehabilitation fail, as they often do in the most disturbed patients, families, friends and even therapists get frustrated and finally turn away with a sense that we have talked with someone who is uncomprehending and beyond help.

To most psychiatrists, such people quickly become "untreatable" if they do not respond to a supportive psychotherapy, antipsychotic medication, halfway houses and day care where cognitive therapy and social skills are practised. Often, such people fall through the cracks and end up in and out of hospitals or extended care facilities, or live homeless on the streets. We are told from early on in medical school that delusions, once fixed, cannot be altered if the standard treatments fail. Such people appear doomed to a life of deterioration and confusion. They don't seem to understand how the world works. Trapped in a purgatory of their own misconceptions, to all intents and purposes they are tortured and lost souls. They join the ranks of the "untreatable".

From the beginning of my psychiatric training, as a medical student on a psychiatry ward, I wondered about our usual modes of treatment of the most severely disturbed patients. It just didn't seem right to approach psychotic people from a purely biological perspective. Not only did such a drug-oriented approach appear superficial, but it left out the essence of the development of the person involved and his capacity for relatedness. It ran counter to my background in honours English, where plot and character development were the subject of immense interest and passionate discussion. I began to ask myself and others questions about what was assumed to be the best care available. I was young and searching. I read everything I could find on schizophrenia, its origins and treatment. I worked on the psychiatric wards at Albert Einstein, where there were many stimulating teachers with perspectives ranging from Freudian to Jungian to existentialist. I spent the better part of my last year at medical school working with Ronnie Laing in London, and lived with psychiatric patients at Villa 21 at Shenley Hospital in nearby Dunstable. I pursued gestalt approaches to psychosis in Berkeley during my internship, and, as military service, spent several years evaluating psychiatric drug efficacy for the National Academy of Sciences in Washington DC, as well as studying in depth psychodynamic approaches to schizophrenic patients at Chestnut Lodge in neighbouring Rockville, Maryland.

From the beginning of my interest in schizophrenia, I thought it was a treatable disorder, if only we could fathom how the person in front of us had slipped into such a perplexing way of being. Even though many in my field thought such patients were beyond any meaningful help, I thought schizophrenia and delusional disorders were eminently understandable, and hence treatable. I liked talking to people who were so disturbed; I found their leaps of logic, their strange associations and their subtle communications to be compelling. Was it my interest in literature and characterisation? Was it the fact that this was the mid-sixties, with all of the attendant seeking and spiritual and philosophical ferment and exploration? My questions to myself and others burgeoned.

Are such patients really "untreatable"? Or have we, as a profession, failed them with a primarily drug-oriented approach? Is it possible that "untreatable" as a concept is an indictment of the mental health profession's lack of a creative approach to such confusion and despair? Are they really lost? Are these allegedly "untreatable" people reachable, if we but modify our usual drug-oriented approach? What would happen if we tried to plumb the nature and extent of their hallucinations and delusional beliefs? What might the result be if we, as committed therapists, entered into the realms of madness, into the thinking of the seemingly hopelessly disturbed person in front of us? Since we could only really understand someone by an empathic connected analysis of his being (Medard Boss' Daseinanalysis), in the process decreasing isolation, could change in delusional beliefs and behaviour occur if we got to the bottom of how such thinking began? What happens if we genuinely try to understand the origin of such psychotic beliefs, even with the most disturbed, and attempt to put together an emotional and historical thread that describes how delusional beliefs or schizophrenic thought began? Would such an inquiry lead to therapeutic and behavioural change? Is it possible that many who have been regarded as "untreatable" can be helped?

By the time I came to Mount Zion Hospital in San Francisco for my psychiatric residency training, I had some pretty clear ideas that it was possible to psychotherapeutically treat the most disturbed patients. There, in Bob Wallerstein's psychodynamic psychotherapy training programme, oriented towards treating the neuroses, I found that a similar approach could also work with schizophrenia and delusional disorders. My questions began to be resolved as I put my ideas into practice. Soon, as the following cases demonstrate, I realised that there was most likely no such thing as an "untreatable" patient, only our lack of a creative approach, limited by therapeutic attitude, interest, finances, and a stable living situation. I began to believe that the concept of "untreatable" was a defensive attitude by my profession, a retreat from difficult and hard-to-reach patients. I had my preconceptions as to what was possible in the psychodynamic psychotherapy of psychosis, and began to put them into practice, with predominantly gratifying results.

I played it by ear. My thinking was supported by readings from many sources, ranging from psychoanalysis to a line from the Bardo of Karmic Illusions in the Evans-Wentz translation of the Tibetan Book of the Dead. " Whatever fearful and terrifying visions thou mayst see, recognize them to be thine own thought forms. I had learned much in my training and had the overriding belief that it was possible to treat even the seemingly incomprehensible. I never knew what would come up, but something usually did. I trusted and honed my therapeutic instincts as I began to see more of other therapists' treatment failures, other psychiatrists' "untreatables". Unsurprisingly, I soon became a psychotherapist of last resort for the most disturbed, for people with schizophrenia or delusional disorders.

Over my more than 35 years of outpatient practice with such seemingly hopeless and "untreatable" people, I have confirmed my preconceptions that even the most chaotic and disturbed schizophrenics could be treated psychotherapeutically. As in Fitzgerald's *Rubaiyat of Omar Khayyam*, I came out "by the same door where in I went". I leave it to the reader to see if the material warrants my assessment.

It is my conviction that a thorough understanding of the origin of the beliefs of the most severely disturbed people via an exploratory intensive psychodynamic psychotherapy, with judicious and appropriate medication as needed, can lead to gradual intrapsychic change, healing and eventual relinquishing of delusional beliefs and schizophrenic thought. The case studies presented in this book will support such a hypothesis. First, though, we must understand a little about delusions and schizophrenic thought. We must peek into the world of those ensnared by their beliefs.

CHAPTER ONE

Delusional reality

A person's behaviour is determined by his conscious and unconscious beliefs. We each have a Weltanschauung, a belief
system that guides us and serves as an internal compass.
Some people have trouble if their convictions conflict with each
other; this is the pain of neurosis. Some have a great deal of trouble
if their beliefs collide with other people's beliefs; here, issues of insecurity and conformity become paramount. Some people stick to their
convictions about generally agreed reality in the face of all evidence
to the contrary; this is the realm of psychosis and delusional belief.

A delusion is a firmly held belief in something false, a belief in
something untrue for the rest of us, a set of ideas and concepts that
guide and predetermine a person's behaviour, without adequate
external corroboration. By definition, a delusion is clung to in the
face of objections and rational arguments from others. Delusions
make it impossible for a person to accurately perceive and function
in day-to-day life.

Delusions occur in a number of different diagnostic categories.
In schizophrenia, where there is a withdrawal of energy from the
external world, auditory hallucinations and diminished social and
occupational functioning often go hand in hand with fixed delu-

1

sional ideas. In paranoid delusional disorder, occupational functioning may persist in the face of bizarre and self-referential ideas which make it extremely difficult to maintain personal relationships. In multiple personality disorder, delusional beliefs about the composition of one's own self make it very hard to function as an integrated being. And of course, mood disorders may have a delusional component ranging from manic, inflated grandiosity and megalomania to the depressive, hypochondriacal and deflated self.

People with delusional beliefs and schizophrenic thought become mired in their own misconceptions and misperceptions, burrowing further into a rigid solipsistic orientation towards life. Psychological energy is withdrawn from the external world of people and things and focused on the internal delusional reality. Internal reality, highly energised or cathected, takes precedence over the world the rest of us live in. Attempts to redirect and reorient a delusional person are often doomed to failure. The pattern of such a person is far more likely to become one of repeated hospitalizations and deterioration. For relatives, friends and therapists, delusional people appear immutably stuck and "untreatable".

Delusional people misperceive and orchestrate events internally in very strange ways that mean little to most of us. Passing cars, a chance glance, a word uttered between two people who have no relationship to the delusional person, all take on specific, idiosyncratic meaning. Words and sounds have unique symbolic and self-referential connotations, as do world events. For such people, anything might mean anything. The colour of clothing, advertisements, and newspaper stories might mean one thing to one delusional person and something quite different to another delusional person. Such a person may be able to carry on conversations but, unbeknown to us, mean something quite different from what we mean. To me a black hat is a black hat, but to the schizophrenic person blackness may be the spur of a train of associations leading to witches or a similar tangent to the shape of the hat and someone in another state who had that shape hat or toolbox. Sometimes the schizophrenic or delusional person is actually filtering everything through third and fourth parties, seen only by him and with whom only he can communicate.

Delusions come in all modalities and forms. There are visual, tactile, olfactory, gustatory, auditory and thought delusions. Some have delusions of persecution, omnipotence, and influence. Others have somatic (bodily) delusions, an extreme form of hypochondria. Depending on one's mood, delusions may be of grandeur, if elated, or self-accusation and remorse, if depressed. There is delusional litigiousness and pathological jealousy. Still others live in worlds populated by long gone or imaginary people.

A person with delusional beliefs might be certain that the sound of a car in the street means that there is a communication to him in that sound. Perhaps he is convinced that a passing person's gesture with the right hand means one self-referential thing; with the left, another. Old movies and television reruns might be speaking in an extremely personal way to the viewer, including him in the dialogue in a way that the movie director never intended when he made the film years before. Day-to-day events and realistic data might be filtered through the medium of a comforting and engaging being, a protector, or through the constant criticisms of an angry, torturing being that no one but the patient can see or hear.

Worlds not readily seen by others are revealed to the delusional patient through the ingenuity and activity of his mind. Newspapers, magazines, television ads, billboards, even the passing words of a pedestrian are reinterpreted. Perhaps one's teeth are wired, one's thoughts monitored, one's every reaction noted by the powers that be in a far distant place. Perhaps machinery or satellites are involved in a constant oversight of one's own thoughts and feelings.

These strange readings of events are of paramount importance. The delusional or schizophrenic person is trying to make sense of the world he lives in. He may do it in bizarre ways, but there is a logic to delusions, if one spends enough time exploring them. Perhaps stimuli are overwhelming; perhaps childhood fears and expectations are placed on seemingly innocuous situations. Perhaps grandiosity is a cover for a feeling of worthlessness; perhaps paranoia is feared retribution for imagined danger or, in other circumstances, punishment for fantasies or actions.

When one is vulnerable to forming delusions, "perhaps" quickly becomes certitude, which becomes a rigid paranoia with no outlet, as misperception builds on fear in a constant attempt to catch up with or get one step ahead of the alleged torturing powers.

A delusion is a creative compromise, albeit unrecognised, on the patient's part. It contains the encoded message; undeciphered, it

wreaks havoc and destruction in the mind and being of the delusional person. It is an extreme, all or nothing solution to emotional
and intrapsychic difficulties.

Some people are vulnerable to forming delusions or hallucinations. Is this the result of a constitutional or genetic defect? In such
people, is the forebrain or the cortex of the brain damaged in some
way? If there is neurological damage, is it congenital or is damage
the result of life's experiences and the subsequent enhancement of
neural pathways of unmodulated anxiety and terror? Does painful
psychological experience lead to a surge of alerting brain chemicals
and the consequent laying down of neural pathways that heighten
fear, with an attendant retreat to delusions and hallucinations as
vain attempts at self-soothing through the creation of imaginary
worlds?

I think this book will answer such questions along the lines of
schizophrenic thought and delusions being the result of the psychological effects of life's experiences. Even if there is some inborn constitutional vulnerability, as opposed to an environmentally induced
one, the same treatment message applies: an intensive psychotherapy
of schizophrenic thought and delusions may lead to an ameliorative,
perhaps curative effect, if we only try.

Rather than using left brain rational thought, the schizophrenic is
overwhelmed by the alleged certainty of right brain intuitive process-
ing. Instead of parsing his or her own productions—ranging from
delusions to hallucinations to bizarre conjectures and apprehensions
which are unrealistic and unwarranted—through a logical left brain
perspective, the psychotic patient affirms the "reality" of his or her
own creations in the face of all evidence to the contrary.

Once one is delusional, there is the propensity to develop all types
of delusions. The small child's belief that she came from outer space
seems innocuous enough; it can, however, lead to delusion formation, should external and internal difficulties in life present themselves. Delusional people have a mindset of unreality, handling life's
difficulties through the medium of wishes and fears they believe in.
Gradually, thoughts, images and mind schemes become more real
than the consensually validated reality in which we all live. Once
one is psychotic, it is a small step to become ensnared by one's own
creative processes, one's delusions and hallucinations, as psychological energy is withdrawn from the generally agreed world we live in

and focused on the internal chaotic world. At this point, the schizo-phrenic or delusional person is mired in the realm of psychosis.

But, like the Rosetta stone or the double helix, fathoming the origin of delusions and schizophrenic thought opens an avenue for tremendous insight into the mind of the delusional patient and gives us the possibility for therapeutic change and healing.

CHAPTER TWO

The psychotherapy of delusional states

I n the field of treating the very disturbed and delusional, there is a long tradition of offering humane environments and understanding psychotherapeutic attitudes that can lead to the melting of psychosis and the dissolution of delusional ideas. This is wonderful when it happens; medication, group and psychotherapeutic support may heal the isolation that leads to withdrawal into delusional beliefs. Unfortunately, fewer and fewer of these humane environments are available. When they are available, little attention is focused on the symbolic meaning of delusions and hallucinations to patients, with the result that schizophrenic and delusional patients are often objectified and treated as the "other". A primarily antipsychotic medication approach furthers the view that psychotic patients are different from us and that their productions have little meaning.

Hopefully, Marius Romme and Sandra Escher's "Hearing Voices Movement", artfully chronicled by Daniel Smith in *Muses, Madmen, and Prophets* (2007), will begin to have an effect on how patients and therapists see hallucinations and delusions. But here too, it will be necessary for patients and therapists to fully comprehend the symbolic meaning of each patient's creative productions, and use antipsychotic medications judiciously, rather than just waiting for the right antipsychotic medication to get rid of the voices.

This book is about those severely disturbed patients who did not respond to the best humane ministrations and who were too ensnared in their delusional beliefs to benefit from the routine practice of psychotherapists and institutions. For these critically ill patients, I suggest a more radical yet (in the long run), conservative approach.

It is the purpose of this book to articulate the position that there is a psychotherapeutic treatment, a simple and time-honoured one, which is useful in treating such schizophrenic and delusional people: take a history of the origin of schizophrenic thought, hallucinations or delusional beliefs, and sit with the person as he or she goes through various therapeutic phases, as both patient and therapist try to make sense of hallucinations and delusions from a psychological perspective, gradually understanding the patient's unique symbolism. It is a corollary of the first principle that such an inquiry will drive a wedge between the patient and his psychotic beliefs. In such a process, psychic energy is gradually taken away from the internal world of delusion and hallucination and returns to where it more naturally belongs, to the world of people and things and external interests.

The process of psychotherapy with delusional patients may, on occasion, be a short one, as the patient quickly grasps the symbolic meaning of his delusions or hallucinations and the feelings underlying such a delusional orientation pour out. Such a resolution is infrequent. More usually, the period of psychotherapy aimed at helping the patient overcome a schizophrenic or delusional orientation will be a long and arduous one, with change measured in infinitesimally small increments. Long intervals of seeming stasis must be tolerated by both patient and therapist in the face of what may appear to be gridlock, if the process is to bear fruit.

It is of the utmost importance that the therapist considers the possibility that schizophrenic thought and delusional beliefs will respond to a psychotherapy oriented towards understanding the symbolic meaning to the patient of delusions and hallucinations, as well as towards discovering, uncovering and elaborating the origin of the distorted beliefs. Therapist and patient must come to understand the confluence of external events and emotional and psychological reactions that led to the formation of delusions and hallucinations. Most importantly, the therapist must realise that there is a "method in this madness". He or she must understand that psychodynamic factors underlie seemingly intractable delusional beliefs.

Delusional people are often in great pain. Yet, for a delusional person it is often easier to believe one is God's chosen spokesman than to feel weak, unloved, fearful, tearful and powerless. For some, it is more acceptable to live in terror of the Mafia than to deal with fears, loneliness and unacceptable impulses that existed from child-hood. It is easier to fear other people's intense sexual interest in oneself, as seen in their every word and gesture, than to deal with one's own lust, sense of worthlessness and fear of rejection.

Treatment itself may become a source of delusions. Even though we know that the treatment setting (the container of psychotherapy) is a safe and comfortable one, delusional people may not view it so. We may represent frightening figures; the office may seem bugged; a conduit to the persecuting outside may somehow appear to be present in our communications. These negative issues need to be unearthed and discovered, then looked at and elaborated upon, if change and progress are to occur.

What is necessary is a two-pronged approach. Of crucial impor-tance is the understanding of the schizophrenic or delusional person's life and a comprehension of the beginning and further development of the psychotic beliefs. Just as important is the simple act of sitting with the frightened, emotional, often unloved self, sensing and feeling and empathically responding to and corroborating accurate readings of the situation between patient and therapist. It is only in this psycho-therapeutic relationship that healing, change and growth may occur.

In this type of uncovering psychotherapy one embarks with the patient on a psychic journey that gradually leads to what Harry Guntrip called "the lost heart of the self" (1968). Here we rest, the patient to mourn past losses and grieve about past abuse or intra-psychic terrors. Imperceptibly, he or she takes solace and comfort in the therapeutic relationship, uncovering and exploring the various beliefs and reasons that played a part in becoming so confused. Little by little, he or she gathers strength through our reliving the emo-tional and psychological causation of his or her disturbance. Slowly, ever so timorously, this previously unsalvageable person emerges from the chrysalis, a sensitive soul beginning the passage back to our consensually agreed reality.

When I first began to encounter such convoluted and fragmented people in medical school, I thought the Alexandrine sword of reality testing would quickly cut through the Gordian knot of such irrational beliefs. It didn't take long for me to realise that this had been tried numerous times before, with the result that patients suffering from such disordered thinking only retreated further into the maze of self-deception, which now might include the perception of an attacking therapist.

Since reality testing didn't cut through the labyrinth of delusional distortion, I began to wonder what would happen if we, as therapists, tried to "walk in the moccasins" of the delusional patient. After all, why would a person act and think in such a way unless it made some kind of sense to him, or he was stuck in something that once made sense? I believed it was essential to take a history of the origin of the delusional beliefs. I began to see that such a gradual therapeutic unwinding of Ariadne's web of disturbed perception, thought and behaviour began to release from delusion people who had been trapped in psychotic thought, even after a number of decades.

The difference appeared to be that the slow process of psychodynamic exploration of the development of delusional beliefs had not been seriously tried before with these people, even though many had had numerous hospitalisations, psychotherapies and trials of medications. Other practitioners had not had the courage of their psychodynamic convictions and had doubted that any serious therapeutic inquiry would bear fruit. They had not travelled with their patients through the numerous twists and turns and detours encountered in an exploratory psychotherapy of delusions. In using this psychotherapeutic approach over the last forty years, I have found that gradually, sometimes ever so slowly, intrapsychic and behavioural change could occur in once lost and delusional patients. This finding however, as demonstrated in the cases set out in this book, runs counter to the current beliefs as to what is possible with such patients.

The psychotherapy of delusional states has become a nearly lost art in this era of antipsychotic medications. Although medication can be very helpful, and at times essential, there are a number of reasons why antipsychotics alone may not help. Some patients hate the side effects, even of the newest antipsychotics with their destructive glucose and lipid metabolism alterations. Some refuse medication for philosophical and delusional reasons. Some, even with antipsychotics, merely go underground, with the persistence of beliefs that preclude intrapsychic change and genuine functioning in reality. For example, a delusional person on antipsychotics may be passing a cup of coffee to a long dead relative while appearing to be in reality with us. At some point, such an unexamined and fragile arrangement may fracture, with the risk of the patient becoming openly psychotic.

If medication as the prime treatment modality does the trick, the patient is better off very quickly. I certainly have seen numerous patients who responded to antipsychotic medication with definitely beneficial effects; such patients are relatively easy to treat. However, none of the patients presented in this book ever found or took enough medication to keep delusional beliefs under control. Some refused to take medication at all, or were reluctant to take enough antipsychotic medication. Others took very high doses of antipsychotics, with little or no diminution of delusional beliefs.

It is not an either-or situation with antipsychotics; they may be extremely helpful, and often essential, for a significant period of time. Sometimes patients have to be maintained on them, if possible on a dose that has been titrated down, as they take a closer look at their delusional thinking. Some of these clinical cases demonstrate that antipsychotics may be lowered for a while and then stopped as delusional thinking recedes and ceases. This is a matter of clinical judgment, not a hard core philosophical position that delusional people need to be on medications for life. Some may have to; others may gradually progress to lowered medication, or none at all.

This book attempts to demonstrate that therapeutic change and healing in patients with chronic schizophrenia or delusional states is possible in an outpatient dynamic psychotherapy. Delusional orientation in a number of diagnostic categories (e.g. schizophrenia, paranoid schizophrenia, paranoia and multiple personality disorder) diminished and sometimes stopped as patients responded favourably, over time, to an interpretive psychotherapeutic exploration of the meaning and function of their delusional thinking.

The process

In the process of this work, a number of factors became evident, as patients gave up their schizophrenic or delusional thinking. Firstly, once a patient has become psychotic, it is easy to become ever more enmeshed in schizophrenic or delusional thought and to elaborate increasingly complex and contorted hallucinations and delusional systems. Secondly, there is the fact that patients have supportive and comforting delusions and hallucinations, as well as threatening and terrifying ones. Whether supportive or threatening psychotic manifestations came first depends on the particular case. Suffice to say that once a person has broken the bounds of reality and accepted a hallucination or delusional thought as reality, they are fair game for a plethora of hallucinations and delusions of every conceivable variety.

A third conclusion derived from understanding the maze of psychotic beliefs reveals that patients may hide positive delusions and hallucinations, not wanting to surrender them to rational enquiry; they prefer the pain of overwhelming and terrifying delusions and hallucinations rather than run the risk of giving up comforting and familiar ones. For most schizophrenic and delusional patients, the familiar, unpalatable as it is, is preferable to the unknown.

Long periods of repeated regressions mean that patients are holding on to delusions and hallucinations that they keep from therapists. It is a kind of shell game, for the patients (almost) honestly believe that they are telling the truth about what goes on in their minds. It is a matter of where one puts one's attention; having given up a long held delusion or series of hallucinations, a patient will say he kind of saw it but didn't think it was important to talk about it. On a deeper level, he knew that to talk about it would have meant giving up something very dear to him.

Giving up delusions and hallucinations in a serious way is characterised by increasingly healthy involvement with external reality and relationships with other people. The lack of this ability to function in the world indicates that the patient remains actively schizophrenic or delusional, no matter how he or she may say they is no longer delusional. He or she change from a delusional or hallucinating state to a non-delusional or non-hallucinating state occurs slowly, as the fragmented inchoate self gradually surfaces. As the process of intensive psychotherapy proceeds, various intrapsychic events happen. Little by little, the schizophrenic or delusional patient ingests, then introjects and eventually incorporates the therapist and a more rational observing attitude. Slowly, in successful psychotherapy of the deeply disturbed, regressions diminish and a more mature perspective begins to take hold.

For the therapist to aid such disorganised patients along the path towards relinquishing a delusional or hallucinatory orientation, he or she must be aware of the circuitous defences and resistances the patient will adopt. The patient wants to stick with the familiar, even if the familiar, a delusional approach to life, isolates and alienates him from meaningful contact with people.

The cases cited in this book were often extremely chronic and viewed as "untreatable". Yet they were able to be treated, not through the usual hodgepodge of drug treatment and reality orientation and support, but through an intensive psychodynamic psychotherapy. As these cases demonstrate, a psychodynamic, exploratory psychotherapy gives patients the chance to achieve Freud's dictum for successful treatment: "Where id was, there shall ego be."

This is where the art of psychotherapy with these most disturbed patients is so important. The therapist must be able to see and gradually work therapeutically with delusions, hallucinations, unconscious meanings, resistances to insights, his own reactions and the patient's transference reactions from the past and to the current changing situation. Since psychotherapy is no longer taught in psychiatric training programmes in the United States, it is necessary for the committed practitioner to get advanced training if he hopes to deal with delusional and schizophrenic patients on more than just a superficial level.

CHAPTER THREE

Causes of a delusional orientation

Some people become delusional when their ability to cope is overwhelmed by mood, intense feeling or drugs. Mind-expanding drugs, manic mood or intense anxiety may speed stimuli to such an extent that the person cannot adequately integrate the sensations and ideas floating through his mind. It becomes impossible to tell when a shadow is a shadow and when it is an attacker. Mania may lead to grandiosity, omnipotence and paranoia. Depressed mood, with the attendant slowing of physical and mental stimuli, may lead to delusions of inadequacy, self-recrimination and hypochondria. For patients whose delusions are secondary to a mood disorder, it is of the utmost importance to try and treat the underlying mood disorder with appropriate antimanic, mood stabilising, antidepressant and tranquillising medications. Psychotherapy is helpful in the reintegration of such patients, but is secondary to treating the underlying mood disorder with appropriate medications. For depressed patients, the armamentarium of antidepressant drugs and augmenting agents should be tried in addition to psychotherapy. In some forms of severe treatment-resistant depression, this combination of drugs and psychotherapy becomes a most important vehicle for change.

Some patients are delusionally psychotic as the result of disordered thinking, and have tried repeated antipsychotic medication and inpatient hospitalisation, with little ameliorating effect. Here an intensive psychotherapy may unearth the origins of a delusional system, and play a much more primary role in treatment. One has nothing to lose and everything to gain using such an approach with patients who have tried everything before, with no success. Throughout such a treatment, one must be ready for all types of exacerbations and remissions of delusional and schizophrenic thought and behaviour.

The patients presented in this book were psychotic as the result of psychological and emotional issues, if healing through an intensive psychotherapy is any barometer as to the causation of delusions and hallucinations. It is important to note that they had to be vulnerable, anxious, desperate, and (unwittingly) ready to adopt a delusional or schizophrenic orientation.

Perhaps some schizophrenic and delusional patients are vulnerable neurologically and constitutionally; others may be so on a psychological basis, as a result of traumatic events. In either situation, brain chemistry and neurological pathways may have changed due to the wash of alerting chemicals that these most anxious patients live with, as they misperceive and overreact to reality. In either case, constitutional or environmental, the same intensive psychotherapeutic approach may work, especially when all else has failed.

There are calming biochemical changes that occur in the course of a dynamic psychotherapy. Susan Vaughan has demonstrated in *The Talking Cure* that brain chemistry changes occur in the course of a healing psychotherapy of neurotic patients. In a similar vein, Brian Koehler (personal communication) is writing a book on the brain chemistry and attendant neurological changes that happen in schizophrenia and other severe disturbances as a result of the flood of chemicals released by profound anxiety; he is further writing about the ameliorative effects of the psychodynamic psychotherapy of schizophrenia on brain chemistry, neuronal pathways and behaviour, with anxiety and the flow of alerting brain chemicals diminishing as a helpful psychotherapy proceeds.

Realising that beneficial biochemical, neuronal and behavioural changes may occur during the course of an intensive psychotherapy of schizophrenia makes it possible to explore the factors leading to psychosis. There have to be reasons—loneliness, fear, impulsiveness, for example—to give up generally agreed reality. When one explores the childhood history, there is a strong likelihood that the patient felt neglected and isolated, or terrified; perhaps there has been sexual or physical trauma. There is a high probability of the creation in childhood of imaginary companions who stayed, or receded for a few years and then returned with delusional force. Had reality been kinder, had they coped better in adolescence, such a return to an inner world peopled with their own creations might have been unnecessary. Perhaps one has a friend whom no one else sees, a friend who developed during the times that were intolerable, when all one had was one's imagination. Perhaps an imaginary friend, created under duress, stays as the only respite and warm relationship in a world which is perceived as cruel and brutal.

Whether overwhelmed by external events or reacting to internal psychological issues, our task is to help the patient calm down sufficiently so that psychotherapy of the delusional state may proceed. Once they are calmer (and some of these people don't become calm for years, no matter what medicines they're given and no matter what modifications of their living situations are made), an understanding of the function of, and necessity for, delusions becomes possible.

CHAPTER FOUR

The method

The psychiatric literature over the last forty years has increasingly emphasised the efficacy of antipsychotic medication and supportive psychotherapy, psychiatric day care and halfway houses in the treatment of schizophrenia. It is often felt that individual psychotherapy is of little or no use; cognitive therapy, antipsychotic medication, group therapy, psychiatric day care, and training in social skills are often the only care offered. Advocates of an intensive, psychoanalytically oriented psychotherapy find themselves on the defensive and are told that the burden of proof is on them to demonstrate that this approach works.

In the hope of generating some fruitful discussion and inquiry into the possibility that there are some schizophrenics and delusional people who respond to an insight-oriented, relatively drug-free, outpatient psychotherapy, I'd like to present twelve case studies—some long, some short—of the successful long-term intensive psychotherapy of schizophrenia and delusional states. These cases demonstrate the usefulness in a primarily outpatient, minimal medication setting, of an intensive, psychoanalytically oriented exploratory psychotherapy of schizophrenia and delusional states. Such a psychotherapy is built upon the cornerstones of a belief in unconscious motivation, the existence of transference, countertransference and resistance in the course of psychotherapy, and the benefits of interpretations of these factors aimed at promoting insight, change and growth.

In such an intensive psychodynamic psychotherapy, an attempt is made to analyse and understand the idiosyncratic meaning to the patient of both delusions and hallucinations. Not only is the symbolic meaning to the patient of the content of delusions and hallucinations explored, but a rigorous attempt is made to try to figure out how, why and when psychotic thinking began, and under what emotional and life circumstances. An attempt is also made to put the patient's psychosis into the perspective of the patient's life and customary ways of living.

Since I view many psychoses as unconscious regressive attempts to evade dealing with psychological conflict, painful reality and intolerable affect, my psychotherapeutic interventions focused on making sense of previously chaotic material such as thought disorder, hallucinations, ideas of reference, delusions, bizarre behaviour and paranoia through clarifications, genetic reconstructions and interpretations of transference, countertransference, resistance and dynamics. The intent of these interventions was threefold. First it was necessary to detoxify terrifying intrapsychic material by making conscious to the patient the symbolic meaning of these phenomena. Then I had to make clear to the patient that these psychotic occurrences were often a defensive retreat from psychological conflict, painful reality and powerful affects. Thirdly, an intensive psychotherapy gives the patient the chance to accept and work through the chaotic feelings of neediness, fear, fury, guilt and despair which often preceded the development of delusions and hallucinations.

CHAPTER FIVE

The history of the psychotherapy of schizophrenia and delusional states

T he conventional wisdom, after May (1968) and Grinspoon (1967), is that antipsychotics, alone or with supportive psychotherapy, are the ideal and most cost effective approach to treating schizophrenia. Without antipsychotic medication, many relapse, even with psychotherapy. Klein states that "the addition of psychotherapy to a drug regimen is of no incremental benefit to schizophrenics" (1980, p. 132). May's study has several flaws, however, since therapists were inexperienced and therapy lasted an average of only 49 sessions. This leaves open the strong possibility that experienced therapists over a much longer course might be more successful in the use of a psychodynamic psychotherapy of schizophrenia.

Grinspoon found that in the psychotherapy of schizophrenics with senior therapists twice weekly over a two-year period, those treated with psychotherapy and antipsychotics (thioridazine) did better than those on psychotherapy and placebo; in addition, he found that they didn't fare as well as the state hospital controls who were treated with high doses of phenothiazines. Over the two-year period, Grinspoon found that those receiving psychotherapy were nearly twice as likely to be living out of the hospital as those treated with a high dose of phenothiazines. In fact, results from the third year of therapy show that patients who remained in psychotherapy continued to improve, leaving the results of this study equivocal. This study too leaves open the question of whether a more prolonged and intensive psychotherapy might better provide help to these most disturbed patients.

Gunderson (1984) highlights some of the difficulties in conducting psychotherapy research in schizophrenia. Although he found that reality-oriented, supportive psychotherapy was at least as effective as exploratory, insight-oriented psychotherapy with schizophrenics on high doses of antipsychotics over a two-year period, he leaves open the possibility that a longer time frame might be employed. In addition, senior therapists often did not have therapy time available when new patients joined the study, and less than one third of the patients remained in their assigned treatment at the end of the two-year study period (Stanton, 1984).

The possibility that longer psychodynamic psychotherapy conducted by experienced clinicians might succeed where it did not in the two-year Gunderson and Stanton study dovetails nicely with Karon's comments on this study (1984). He questions the fact that patients in both the supportive and the insight-oriented groups received about the same amount of antipsychotics, with no apparent attempt made to titrate down and stop medication. Karon raises the possibility that continuing antipsychotic medication may have resulted in diminishing affect, and hence run counter to working through material in therapy. He further questions the patients' mean Wechsler IQ of 98.2, wonders if more intelligent patients might have done better in insight-oriented therapy, and raises concerns about why so many patients dropped out of the study and where they went.

Rather than settling the issue of supportive vs. insight-oriented psychotherapy in favour of antipsychotic medication and supportive psychotherapy, the Gunderson and Stanton study raises a number of questions. Could insight-oriented, exploratory psychotherapy with antipsychotic medication gradually titrated down and then stopped succeed in the hands of psychiatrists experienced in the long-term treatment of schizophrenic productions and affect? Do more intelligent patients do better in insight-oriented psychotherapy, as we assume is the case in the psychotherapy of less disturbed patients?

With analyses of neurotic patients lasting five to ten years, why is two years the magic cut-off period for evaluating the efficacy of intensive psychodynamic psychotherapy in far more disturbed patients? Could the oft-repeated assertion that there is no further need for research on the intensive individual psychotherapy of schizophrenia (Klerman, 1984) be somewhat premature?

Even though antipsychotic medication has been one of the main factors in the sharp decrease in state hospital populations, little can be done to keep people on medicines once they are discharged from the hospital. Once released from the hospital, a number of patients refuse to take medicines, and so run the risk of joining the homeless. These wandering mentally ill are a testament to the difficulties of a primarily drug-oriented approach.

Antipsychotic medicines may be very helpful: if they work and the patient will tolerate them, schizophrenic and delusional symptoms may abate. But many patients will not take these antipsychotic medicines, or receive little benefit from them. A number of patients raise questions as to the quality of their life on medicines, and stop taking them. Although tardive dyskinesia (Crane, 1973) is rarely a side effect of the newer atypical antipsychotics, some delusional people hate the serious glucose and lipid metabolism side effects (as well as lesser ones), and stop medication.

There is also an increased and prolonged dependency on mental health services in patients on long-term antipsychotic regimens. Bockoven and Solomon (1975) contrasted a patient group seen prior to the use of the antipsychotics with a patient group seen when the major tranquilizers were in general use in the 1970s. The earlier, pre-drug group was less dependent (over a five year period) on mental health services and showed increasing initiative and independence.

A recent study by Harrow and Jobe (2007) came to the conclusion that not all schizophrenics need to use antipsychotics throughout their lives. They found that "a larger percent of schizophrenia patients not on antipsychotics showed periods of recovery and better global functioning" than did those patients on antipsychotics.

Finally, delusional patients often believe that strong affects and fantasies are unacceptable and conclude that the prescription of antipsychotic medicines means that the psychiatrist and patient have reason to fear and suppress these powerful feelings and intrapsychic processes. Antipsychotic medicines may further the view that the patient has to keep his demons under control even in psychotherapy, and that antipsychotic medicines offer the only route for achieving this "demon control".

There has been a multiplicity of approaches to treating schizophrenia and delusional states, ranging from milieu (Jones, 1953) to family (Ackerman, 1958) to direct analysis (Rosen, 1962) to rebirthing (Laing, 1976) and cognitive therapy. In addition, there have been treatments originating in various psychoanalytically oriented schools as diverse as Sullivan (1962), Klein (1948), Jung (1960) and Freud (1911). These differing analytic vantage points are used for conceptual understanding, however; antipsychotic medication, day care, halfway houses and supportive psychotherapy are all too often the general rules of treatment.

The psychoanalytically derived treatments of schizophrenia devolve into two major approaches: supportive, based upon a view of schizophrenia as a deficit disease (Vic Calef's "they just don't have the tickets"), and insight-oriented, based upon a view of schizophrenia as a retreat from intrapsychic conflict and intolerable affect. Although Schlesinger (1969) points out that "support is one of the essential purposes of all psychotherapy", these two different orientations lead to two very different therapeutic strategies.

It is of course possible that some schizophrenics are best viewed from the perspective of deficit and others from the perspective of retreat from intrapsychic conflict. Yet all the patients described in this book responded, to one extent or another, to interpretations centering on flight from psychological pain, intrapsychic conflict, overwhelming reality and powerful affects.

Perhaps patients who develop delusions are predisposed to do so, genetically or environmentally. Perhaps they have been isolated or neglected or traumatised in childhood. Perhaps they did reasonably well, and then were overcome by a painful life experience such as immigration or divorce. Perhaps they have lost friends or loved ones or some other form of security. In these previously predisposed people, life events may take on such painful meanings that they unconsciously retreat into a world of delusions.

Since previously "untreatable" patients responded to a psychodynamic and uncovering approach, I have to wonder if those who view schizophrenia as a deficit disorder just haven't gone far enough in their work with these patients. Could one man's deficit disorder be another man's—a psychodynamic psychotherapist's—way station to an understanding of the resistances that prevent healing in even seemingly hopelessly delusional and schizophrenic patients?

Those advocating a reality-oriented, supportive therapy view schizophrenics as suffering from a deficit disease (Wexler, 1971), either constitutional or developmental. According to them, this deficit leads to an inadequate repressive barrier and eventual decathexis of internal objects (Freud, 1915) during periods of overwhelming stress. This approach leads to a "real relationship", reality testing, antipsychotic drug use, occasional working in the transference and role playing in an attempt to mitigate harsh, destructive superego introjections. At its worst, it may lead to excesses such as those of Ferenczi, who in his rapport therapy hugged patients to make up for any purported lack of early positive mothering.

Those advocating an insight-oriented approach are rooted in Freud's finding that conflict with reality was important in the development of psychosis and the withdrawal of psychic energy from the external world to the internal world of delusions and hallucinations (Freud, 1894). Klein (1948) and Rosenfeld (1965) emphasize the importance of early infancy in the development of splitting and projective identification. Arlow and Brenner (1964) see schizophrenia as a defensive retreat from intrapsychic conflicts. Boyer (1971, 1967) interprets the defensive aspects of psychotic productions as an attempt to flee anger and oedipal conflicts in an outpatient analytic setting. Guntrip (1968) interprets pre-oedipal conflicts and yearnings, emphasising a ubiquitous desire to flee relationships and retreat to womb-like safety rather than confront a fearful, often unrewarding world and the intensity of one's own fears, needs and fury at needs not met. Bion (1962) focuses on pathological projective identification. Kohut (1971) emphasizes the necessity to be empathically available to even the most psychotic. Fromm-Reichmann (1950) emphatically states: "With the schizophrenic, interpretation of dynamics and genetics is the approach needed."

Often, as a number of these cases demonstrate, previous supportive psychotherapy has not affected the underlying psychodynamics, leaving the patient in the continued throes of his own distortions and projections. Viewed from another perspective, in supportive psychotherapy the patient's anger, greed and unfulfilled needs turn sour any proffered emotional sustenance, leaving both patient and therapist in a quandary. Searles (1975) maintains: "Those [...] who view schizophrenia as predominantly a deficiency disease are needful of maintaining under repression the bad mother components of their identities and of seeking to reaffirm, in their attempted warm and giving approach to the schizophrenic patient, their own good mother aspects."

As these case accounts demonstrate, the patient's trust in the therapist and in his reliability as a consistent object, although extremely important, is not sufficient by itself to help the patient through the morass of delusions and psychosis. Supportive therapists believe that the gradual development of positive superego introjections will diminish the archaic, denigrating, critical introjections that generally occur in schizophrenia. In practice, however, as a number of these cases demonstrate, a previous supportive psychotherapy is likely to leave untouched an essentially psychotic stance of delusion and projection onto external reality of inner thought processes. Although heroic efforts were made in previous supportive therapies, clinical improvement occurred only when a more interpretive, psychoanalytically oriented approach was attempted.

All the patients presented in this book were previously diagnosed as delusional or schizophrenic by other psychiatrists and/or hospitals, and fulfilled the criteria for the diagnosis of delusional disorder or schizophrenia (Carpenter et al., 1973). Some were schizophrenic on psychological testing as well. One was suffering from a severely delusional Multiple Personality Disorder. Yet they responded to an interpretive, dynamically oriented psychotherapy.

In Laing's metaphor (1960), Freud gave us the theory of the unconscious, Perseus' shield, with which even the very disturbed may be psychotherapeutically led to confront the Medusa of psychosis. In such a therapeutic process, the patient begins to gain increasing ego strength and the capacity for self-observation.

Boyer (1983), Guntrip (1961), Fromm-Reichmann (1959), Sechehaye (1951), Will (1968), Lidz (1973), Winnicott (1958), Pao (1979), Giovacchini (1979) and many others have added much to our understanding of the dynamics and treatment of these allegedly "untreatable" schizophrenic and delusional patients. Fleck (1985), commenting on the term "untreatable" found in a book on treating schizophrenics (Stone, 1983), aptly and poignantly states: "Many patients in the public sector, probably the majority, have become 'untreatable' because they have not experienced treatment adequate to their needs."

In the United States, there has been a profound swing over the last forty years to the use of antipsychotic medication, supportive psychotherapy and psychiatric day care in the treatment of overtly psychotic patients. This seems to me to be an extreme treatment approach. It is my sense that other countries, particularly the Scandinavian ones, have a better track record of treating the most disturbed people. Perhaps in these countries a mix of social and supportive psychotherapies returns patients to home and the community in better shape than in the United States, where the art of psychotherapy is no longer taught or valued in psychiatric training programmes. In other countries, the art of psychotherapy—even of the most disturbed patients—may be faring better.

For the practising therapist or the reader interested in a more in-depth conceptualisation of various therapeutic strategies for treating schizophrenic and delusional patients, as well as a further understanding of intrapsychic processes and theories of treatment, I can recommend a number of books I have found useful over the years. In addition, there are numerous clinicians and theoreticians who have shed much light on the psychotherapy of schizophrenia, but I will leave a more thorough elaboration of all those involved in developing a theoretical basis for the psychotherapy of schizophrenia to a more scientific volume.

Harry Guntrip's *Schizoid Phenomena, Object Relations and the Self* and Harold Searles' *Collected Papers on Schizophrenia and Related Subjects* rank high on my list, as do Ping-Nie Pao's *Schizophrenic Disorders*, Bryce Boyer and Peter Giovacchini's *Psychoanalytic Treatment of Schizophrenic and Characterological Disorders*, Frieda Fromm-Reichmann's *Principles of Intensive Psychotherapy* and Bert Karon and Gary Vandenbos' *Psychotherapy of Schizophrenia*.

Ronnie Laing's *Divided Self* and *The Self and Others*, John Gunderson and Loren Mosher's *Psychotherapy of Schizophrenia*, Murray Jackson's *Weathering the Storms: Psychotherapy for Psychosis* and *Unimaginable Storms: A Search for Meaning in Psychosis*, Jim Grotstein's *Splitting and Projective Identification*, Marguerite Sechehaye's *Symbolic Realization* and Tom Ogden's *The Primitive Edge of Experience* might round out some seminal selections that will guide the serious student of the psychotherapy of schizophrenia along his or her way.

If you are interested in a more detailed history of the psychotherapeutic treatment of schizophrenia and delusional disorders, buttressed by scientific studies of the efficacy of the psychotherapy of schizophrenia, I refer you to the Appendix, where my colleague Brian Koehler has allowed me to include his postings on these subjects from the website of ISPS, the International Society for the Psychological Treatments of the Schizophrenias and other Psychoses. ISPS is a worldwide organisation dedicated to the humane and psychological treatment of schizophrenia and delusional disorders, and is an excellent forum for the latest ideas on how to treat such severely disturbed patients.

CHAPTER SIX

Psychotherapeutic technique and stages in the psychotherapy of delusional states

I n patients who are chronically delusional or schizophrenic, and have been so for many years, psychotherapy has many phases. First there is an attempt to assess the situation and see when the psychotic material began. Next is the requirement to try to reality test, and when that fails (as is likely), to try and understand the need for delusions or hallucinations, and when and how they became apparent. Such an approach will lead through many turns and curves, detours and crevices as we go deeper into the origin of psychosis. At some time historically, we reach the point where delusional belief or hallucinations began. Perhaps it was to diminish loneliness or assuage terror. Perhaps it's a chthonic, preverbal pain beyond all articulation, from which the patient is attempting to flee via restitutive imaginary friends.

In the course of our work, the feeling states of sadness, terror, loneliness, or depression will be experienced by the delusional patient. Gradually we begin to see how it all began, and slowly we provide a road map of our understanding to the patient. Comprehending the origin of delusions and schizophrenic thought is important. To reconstruct the feelings and choices of the child or young adult who adopts (or is forced into) a delusional or schizophrenic orientation is quintessential.

But more is required than our intellectual understanding. Since we are dealing with the most tender, terrified, sad aspects of another's being, the psychotherapeutic working through of resistances and defences is paramount. Eventually, if we keep our wits and our intuition about us, we reach a wounded core. If we are attuned, we empathically bear witness to, contain, and start the healing process of the undefended, vulnerable person sitting with us.

Defences — movement, dissociation, projection, distraction, displacement, to name a few — are primary in any psychotherapy of delusional states. These defences seem necessary from the patient's point of view. Our task is to deal with the defences in the transference relationship — past ways of seeing, intuiting and reacting which are played out in the container of psychotherapy — as in life at large. Our goal is to finally help the patient to sit with his own being — his rage, yearning, neediness, terrors and fantasies — as we sit with ours, in a relatively undefended way. Only then can calmness ensue and healing begin.

Dealing with issues in the transference is a simple concept, but one that requires an ongoing observation of both patient (transference) and therapist (countertransference) reactions and fantasies. It lies at the heart of all dynamic psychotherapy and requires the understanding on the therapist's part that patients have unconscious motivation and resistance to change, and that they have defences to maintain the status quo, painful as it is.

Therapist reactions and over-reactions (countertransference) often occur in the course of working with such chaotic patients, and need to be constantly observed and analysed. One therapist told me how she tried to comfort her chronically disturbed patient with a hug at the end of the session. The hug was totally out of character for this therapist and hid her anger at the patient for his constant demands for more time. Once this countertransference was understood and dealt with by the therapist, therapy could proceed to a more healing interaction.

Crucially important is the knowledge — to be gleaned through repeated interactions — that even psychotic patients transfer the past onto the present and repeat past developmental stages and interactions in their relationships, delusions and schizophrenic productions. If anything, the psychotic patient's transference reactions are more dramatic and extreme. As such, they must be worked through with the psychotherapist's knowledge that even these powerful and at times troubling reactions can be dealt with by the usual therapeutic technique of exploring and dynamically understanding these intense phenomena.

Gradually, delusional and schizophrenic patients become aware that they are the creators of their psychotic productions. Little by little, projected and feared impulses that took the form of hallucinations and delusions become understandable and detoxified. The sense of being acted on by others becomes a central theme to explore. As the understanding of issues in the transference proceeds, the patient begins to see how he or she transfers and projects onto the therapist all types of feelings—from fear to disgust to indifference to love to yearning to hate. In one so disturbed, more powerful feelings from the unremembered but emerging past may occur, ranging from terror to murderous rage to inchoate dependence and the desire to merge, scoop out, possess and be possessed. In addition, one must keep one's observational therapeutic eyes open to the possibility of the emergence in the transference of hallucinated voices, sounds, smells, body parts and presences, all of which appear real to the patient, and all of which have meaning as the story unfolds.

It is crucial to recognize that people become delusional for a number of different reasons and at different psychological developmental points. Delusional orientation is the result of the interaction of environment, genetics, psyche and the developmental stage at the time of insult. As therapists, we have to be cognisant of the often rapidly shifting developmental stages we are dealing with in a person so primitive. We must anticipate, understand and withstand the rage of the fearful paranoid defending himself against his own projected fears, desires and fantasies. We must empathically sense and therapeutically comfort, gradually making clear the origin of such behaviour to the often regressed person who feels that the world is overwhelming and that retreat to womb-like safety is his only option.

Delusional and hallucinating people are over the edge, and hence often regarded as "untreatable". For most therapists, these paranoid schizophrenics, chronic schizophrenics, or fully fledged multiple personality disorders are psychotic and too disturbed to be given more than supportive help. Supportive help generally entails medication, reality testing, socialising patients, living situations and trying to get them to work; it does not include an intensive, exploratory psychotherapy aimed at getting to the bottom of the difficulty and helping the person reintegrate psychologically and then socially.

What I am proposing to demonstrate through a number of case illustrations of severely disturbed schizophrenic and delusional people, even those considered "untreatable" by other therapists and institutions, is that an intensive exploratory in-depth psychotherapy, judiciously using whatever medications are appropriate, can lead to lasting psychological change, development and healing in even the most disturbed and delusional patients.

Where previous supportive psychotherapies failed, leaving unchanged an essentially psychotic and delusional orientation towards life, an intensive psychotherapy—exploring and understanding resistances, defences, the origin of delusional beliefs, and the symbolic meaning to the patient of his or her productions—gives the patient the hope of altering a deteriorating and life-threatening course. With the deciphering of delusions and the symbols contained in delusions, hallucinations, and the schizophrenic orientation, feelings and emotions which have been dammed up for years will flow, often with a terrorising effect for the patient. This is the time for the therapist to be aware of suicidal propensities. It is crucial that once delusions are unwoven, the underlying feelings must be dealt with in the container of therapy.

Colleagues tell me that I make it sound too simple. It is, and it isn't, simple. What is required on the therapist's part is the knowledge that it is possible to peel the onion of psychosis, eventually arriving at the kernel of self-hood and chaotic and threatening feelings. It is further necessary that the therapist of such disturbed people be aware that the transference-countertransference issues that arise in the course of dealing with delusional people will be extremely intense, and that they will resolve over time by following the four-fold path of exploring, understanding, containing and working through the various intrapsychic and transferential issues that arise. Such a belief in the healing power of the work we do allows the committed therapist the ability to tolerate the slow pace, frustration and countertransference issues that will almost certainly arise. Our goal is the possibility, in the long run, of a person emerging from the web of delusional misperception.

These cases will hopefully buttress the belief and commitment of therapists who embark on the long journey to loosen and finally melt the internal shackles that lock the deluded in madness. I believe that you, the reader, will see that an in-depth psychodynamic exploration of delusions and schizophrenia may lead to healing and cure where psychosis and the concept of "untreatable" previously reigned.

Apologia and clinical presentation

A t the risk of issuing testimonials for myself and this intensive psychotherapeutic approach, I would like to present a number of reasonably successful case examples demonstrating the efficacy of an intensive psychodynamic psychotherapy in patients suffering from schizophrenia or delusional disorder. Of course, not every patient will respond to this intensive psychotherapeutic approach. Some may bolt from treatment, either as a transference reaction or as an acting out of their psychosis. Would that they had stayed and had the chance to reap the benefits of an intensive psychotherapy of psychosis, as did the patients described in this book.

My purpose is twofold. Clearly I want to demonstrate the effectiveness of an intensive psychotherapy in even the most disturbed schizophrenic and delusional patients. In addition, these tales may serve as hortatory teaching illustrations and help to provide courage and the outline of a game plan to therapists willing to work in the realms of madness. I hope the examples speak for themselves.

The identifying characteristics of patients have been changed in the interests of confidentiality.

CHAPTER SEVEN

The Good Angel, the Bad Devil, the Smiling Man's Voice, and Mother-God

J udith was a tall, thin, blonde woman in her early twenties when I first met her, while I was working in a psychiatric emergency room. Her much loved psychiatrist, whom she had seen for five years, was on holiday. She had cut herself four times prior to coming to the emergency room.

When she explained what had happened, and I had taken appropriate medical action (for these were more than superficial cuts), I asked why she had cut herself. She had no idea. Did the number of cuts (four) have any significance for her? Were there any feelings going through her prior to and at the time of cutting herself? She stopped short and looked perplexed: for whatever reason she was not accustomed to exploring the meaning of her behaviour. She hadn't questioned, merely acted.

She quickly began to wonder what she had been doing and why she had been acting so strangely. The number four meant four years old to her. Did such an age mean anything to her? Judith didn't know. And underlying feelings? She responded with the obvious, that she was angry that her therapist was away. Why cut? Again, she didn't know, but it was a release of her feelings.

In our short interview, my approach of trying to decipher the psychological origins of her cutting herself and attempting to make sense of previously unexamined actions was so different from the supportive handholding treatment she was accustomed to that she began to discuss with her therapist and parents the idea of beginning treatment with me. Several months later, when the treating psychiatrist concurred, she began a more exploratory insight-oriented psychotherapy with me which revealed much more clearly what her thinking was and how it arose.

The previous therapist had viewed her as essentially psychotic and in need of supportive care, for she had several diagnoses of acute (now chronic) schizophrenia on both psychiatric assessment and psychological testing. In addition, there had been several months-long hospitalisations at three different psychiatric hospitals, five years of daily supportive individual and group therapy sessions, protracted courses of numerous antipsychotic medications at extremely high doses, and (as if things weren't bad enough already) a traumatic course of electroconvulsive therapy (shock treatment) before she had finished college.

I guess the rationale for this last treatment in one so young and with such a diagnosis was to drive the psychosis out, as the inventor of ECT, Ugo Cerletti, thought he had done with his first patient, a hallucinating schizophrenic, who told him the voices were gone after his first unanaesthetised convulsion with ECT. (To me it sounds as if Cerletti's patient didn't want to have another painful seizure at Cerletti's hands.) The treatment didn't drive Judith's psychosis out, however. It did serve to further terrify her, not only because it is such a barbaric treatment for this diagnosis and age group but also because they failed to fully anaesthetise her for at least one treatment.

Such a "supportive" treatment approach is anything but supportive of the individual. It is a warehousing approach, attempting to cover over the symptoms and disordered thinking. Sometimes it works and the psychosis goes into remission; sometimes it doesn't. With Judith, the "supportive" approach had failed terribly, no matter how much medication she took or how much reality-oriented activity she was involved in. Nowhere in this previous approach with Judith was there the possibility for self-understanding, other than to say that these are delusions or hallucinations and she should keep them to herself.

Judith was the eldest child of a prosperous businessman from another city. The father was stern and preoccupied with business, yet caring. The mother was supportive and overly indulgent. When Judith was an infant, her mother had enlarged the hole in the teat of the baby bottle, so that the child would get her milk more quickly (and the mother would have to deal with less noise and difficulty). Until the age of three, her mother put her to bed early every night with bottles of juice; since Judith wasn't tired, she remembers fantasising for what seemed like long periods until she fell asleep. Still later, her mother let her stay at home from kindergarten for six months, when she inexplicably appeared terrified about leaving her mother and began vomiting at school.

Judith had a three and a half years younger brother. She remembers hating her brother, who got so much more attention than she did. Her father's parents died before her birth; her maternal grandfather committed suicide just before she turned six, and her maternal grandmother died while she was in college.

Haltingly, she told me over the first few months of psychotherapy, as I enquired into her thoughts and preoccupations, a fact she had hidden from her previous therapist: she had a "Good Angel" who lived just over her right shoulder. This "Good Angel" was a woman, dressed in white flowing robes as any good angel should be. For years the angel, whom she could see and hear, had dictated to her what she should do. She would converse with this presence, even though she might be talking to other people. This accounted for the engrossed daydreaming look and flattened affect that had been noted about her for years—had no one seriously attempted to ask about where her attention went during this obvious withdrawal from day-to-day reality? Unfortunately, the answer was that no therapist had asked what she was thinking about when she appeared to be internal and preoccupied.

The "Good Angel" told her to do things that were, to her mind, "good" for her, such as cutting her wrists. The "Good Angel" had persisted since early adolescence, when she had told Judith to cut herself, and she had carved "HURT" on her abdomen. She couldn't tell the psychiatrist she was seeing then about the reasons she had cut herself. Perhaps she was embarrassed; perhaps questions about delusional thinking were not raised, for the general tendency among most practitioners has been to assume that nothing can be done with

such disordered thinking apart from covering it over with antipsychotic medications and supportive care.

Gradually she elaborated her history with the "Good Angel".
Having persisted for a number of years, the "Good Angel" was her
master. When she cut herself, took overdoses or threatened to jump
from the Golden Gate Bridge, she was following the precepts of her
Lord. These seemingly self-destructive acts were "good" things to do
to herself, for she was "such a terrible person", and had been so for
nearly as long as she could remember, certainly back to kindergarten. She had known she was "such a terrible person" since then, even
before the "Good Angel" had developed. At this point, during the first
six months of psychotherapy, she didn't know why she believed she
was "such a terrible person"; she just knew she was. I asked her about
her badness, wondered why she felt so terrible and thought so ill of
herself. For her it was a given that she was bad or evil, since the "Good
Angel" told her so. She had no sense as to why this might be the case.

I began to cast doubt on the "Good Angel" who wanted her to
hurt herself and be punished. I questioned how "good" could have
such negative consequences. I inquired as to how a "good" angel
could urge her to do such self-destructive things. I began to ask a lot
of questions and wondered if there were, in fact, angels. Could her
belief in angels be a relic of her early religious upbringing? How did
the angel begin?

This is a delicate time in any psychotherapy, for it is important to
maintain what is called a working alliance with a patient. How do
you do this when you are essentially telling someone that they are
mistaken? I find that the best way is to take a history from the delusional figure.

In this situation, I asked Judith to tell me what the "Good Angel"
was saying to her, since I couldn't see or hear it. How did she
develop, and in what circumstances? Judith was extremely vague
about the origin of her protecting demiurge, and could say only that
she began saying "such a terrible person" in early high school. Judith
didn't remember any particular thoughts or feelings, sexual or otherwise, at that time. My suspicion was that the "Good Angel" was a
symbolic reaction to the upwelling of sexual feelings during puberty,
but Judith, in her vagueness, thought not. My hope was that the questioning itself would begin to drive a wedge into her firm conviction
of the "Good Angel's" existence and beneficence to her.

Gradually, during the course of the first year of outpatient therapy, she told me she had developed another being, this time a "Bad Devil" who lived over her left shoulder and wanted her to do things that were "bad" for her, such as enjoying herself, having friends, going to school, working, masturbating and developing relationships. We talked about whom the "Bad Devil" might represent. Slowly she was able to understand that it represented me, or a more positive internal aspect of herself. This became confusing, because she was under the sway and domination of the "Good Angel" who wanted her to be punished.

If punishment was good and enjoyment bad, she must be very mixed up and bewildered. If good was bad and bad was good, her psychological life had been turned inside out. Her psychological life was so upsetting to her that it had been placed outside herself in the personages of angels and devils.

There are many layers to the psyche, especially in a severely disturbed and delusional person. Normally we talk of an intrapsychic life, but not yet in this situation. She projected her own superego values (conscience) and impulses outside herself and concretised them in the visual but believed metaphor, hence delusion, of angel and devil. In addition, she exteriorised good and bad and switched them in the process.

These issues were explored in four times weekly psychotherapy in order to help her get a handle on the emerging material. There was much suicidal ideation and some cutting, which was seen to be her difficulty accepting feelings and dealing with the psychological changes required in beginning to look at her self-destructiveness and her belief in the "Good Angel" who was bad for her.

During that first year of treatment, there were a few short hospitalisations to protect her from self-destructively carrying out the "Good Angel's" edicts. This was done for Judith's own good and also served the function of reality testing; the wishes of the "Good Angel" were bad and would be dealt with accordingly. I became the powerful figure who entered her psychic life not just as the "Bad Devil", but as a new protector to protect her from the previous "protector" who actually harmed her.

Little by little her confusion clarified, and she reintegrated during her first year of therapy with me, gave up both "Good Angel" and "Bad Devil", and returned home for a year and a half, where she worked at a paid job. She had stopped hurting herself, came in to therapy once every week or two, and started developing friendships both at home and in San Francisco. As I try to with most patients, I had gradually been lowering her antipsychotic medicines, which were now at a level of about a fifth of what she had previously been taking.

Sounds pretty good, hmmm? But even then I knew better. So often in psychotherapy, especially in working with creative people who have unwittingly constructed a delusional reality, there is much more to the story. This was just the tip of the iceberg. Underneath lurked a delusional system far more serious, pervasive and debilitating than the superficial layer we had addressed.

After a year and a half at home, Judith felt stronger, and returned to San Francisco. She came in and told me in a very uncharacteristic and assertive way that she would no longer take antipsychotic medication, that she wanted to get to the bottom of what had been going on with her, and that she had the sense that the medicines got in the way. So much had been covered over during her earlier therapies by medication and the attitude of previous therapists. She felt so much better trying to understand what was going on with her, as she had increasingly begun to do during the time we had worked together, that she insisted on stopping the antipsychotics. I went along with her desire to stop taking antipsychotics with the proviso that should I feel it necessary, I would reinstate them or hospitalize her. Neither has been necessary for more than thirty years.

After several sessions on no medication, she lay on the floor and began writhing around. After a suitable time, I asked her what this was about. She said she was giving birth.

"To whom?"

"To myself."

After several more minutes of various contortions which were her imagined attempts at negotiating the birth canal, Judith became still. After a little time, she dramatically and bombastically stated, "I'm now born in a new way. Nine months from now is my birthday. [It was.] Nine months from now, I will decide if I will live or die." Gamy, provocative, enticing. It was all these things. And it was more.

The assertiveness and bombast were different from her usual way of being. I asked what was going on and how she had been born. She responded in what seemed to me to be a parody of a little girl's voice that she was four and a half years old, three feet tall, and her name was Judy: "That's what my big sister calls me." To top this off, she told me she was wearing a pink checked dress.

I reality tested with Judith at this point, telling her that as far as I was concerned she was this mid-twenties woman sitting here with me. Perhaps this was her way or describing feeling states or historical information she had trouble dealing with. How had she got the sense that she was two beings, one older and one so much younger? Had she read anything, or seen any movies or television shows? She said no, this was how it had almost always been. Rather than argue with her, and run the risk of cutting off the flow of material, I listened to "Judy's" tale.

"Judy" was in thrall to "Mother-God," a vague white-robed controlling figure who had existed for as long as "Judy" had. "Mother-God" told Judy what to do in a combination of ways. First she fed "Judy", especially by bottle feeding. This comforted "Judy" and pointed her in the right direction, at least as far as what "Mother-God" wanted "Judy" to do. Secondly, "Mother-God" constantly muttered to herself that "Judy" was "such a terrible person". "Judy" was unsure what she had done wrong, but knew she had to do the right thing in order that "Mother-God" would protect her and feed her.

Work was done on the projected nature of "Mother-God" (harsh, punitive, yet nurturing concretisation of a superego in the form of a god-like mother) and "Judy" (the embodiment of a regressive, dependent self, feeling the need for protection), but to little avail. As far as Judith was concerned, she was primarily "Judy" and related events from the past from her view of a young child's perspective; at times, if asked, the "Mother-God" self would chime in with additional material.

Judith had been a precocious little girl, playing the piano to some extent by the age of three. Even though her father was removed and guilt-inducing, she knew that he cared for her. She remembers her pregnant mother at the age of three and her mother giving birth when she was three and a half. She recalls, as "Judy", her little brother being fed, and remembers an aunt nursing an infant at about the same time. A beatific smile spreads across her face as she describes the feeling of warmth and satisfaction fleeting across her cousin's face while she nursed.

Rather quickly she began to resent her little brother, who got all that attention just because he "had that little thing on him". She began to fantasise, at about the age of four, that his penis would be cut off with her mother's sewing scissors, or chopped up like those carrots her mother chopped for soup. She reasoned that if he didn't have a penis, he wouldn't get all that attention. She had these fantasies mainly when she was sent to bed early; they caused her no difficulty. She hated her baby brother, and wanted him dead. She knew even at that age, around four, that these were only wishes and not real.

One day, at the age of four and a quarter, her mother tripped while carrying her little brother, breaking his leg. "Judy" felt responsible for the harm to her brother. Suddenly "Mother-God" emerged in her consciousness, critical and blaming. At this point "Judy" felt very guilty and did an even more serious intrapsychic split between her real self who had wished harm to her little brother and her surface self.

As "Judy" saw it, her angry, resentful wishes towards her brother caused her mother to fall, breaking her brother's leg. She became terrified of her thoughts, fearing that her thoughts and wishes had an effect in the world. This omnipotence and sense of guilt was furthered by her mother saying that she didn't know how she had fallen in the first place. Judy felt that she was at fault for the fall.

Not only did she personify her guilt in the reified form of "Mother-God", she invented a new being, the "Monster". The "Monster" was angry and wanted to eat or masturbate. It was the "Monster" who wanted her brother dead; it was the "Monster", not Judy, who caused her mother's fall. Very quickly it became clear to me (though not to her) that the "Monster" was the repository of all of her unacceptable impulses and sensual feelings. Of course she was explaining all this to me years later, and her memories were clearly filtered through time and many layers of experience. The "Monster" was her way of projecting responsibility, blame and guilt outside her sense of herself. Instead of one person, "Judy", who wished harm to her brother, she quickly turned herself into three.

"Judy" and "Mother-God" formed an alliance which had persisted for the years since. Like the little kid who raids the refrigerator and then says "'Piggy' did it, not me", Judith was not responsible in her mind for thoughts or actions. As the years passed, any sexual or aggressive impulse was laid at the door of the "Monster". As time went on, "Judy" would feed the "Monster" to placate and dull her, while "Mother-God" would say "calories don't count."

Several issues were clearer. Judith didn't like to be responsible. In addition, she was highly self-suggestible, and had escaped real and imagined responsibility over the years by believing such a strange and convoluted intrapsychic scenario. The question was why. Why would someone become so deluded? Could the factors we knew about account for her world view? We knew of the mother enlarging the hole in the baby bottle, so her tendency was to not tolerate frustration. She had wished harm to her brother, and harm had happened to him. Was that enough to lead to such disordered thinking?

I listened to her thoughts and feelings, personified in these different beings, questioning her need to present material in this fashion. Could other issues be responsible for the tripartite splitting of her sense of self? She was adamant. This was how things really were to her, even though I saw her as Judith, a young woman who had long ago split herself into three in a shell game in which the goal was the avoidance of responsibility. We went over this material repeatedly; she remained convinced that she was three beings.

At that point in the treatment I shelved the issue, as we had about two months before her birthday, and she had told me that this birthday could be her death day. I asked Judith what she had decided to do about staying alive. She was furious with me, screaming indignantly, telling me she hated me, as she said she had decided to kill herself and hoped I had forgotten. More precisely, the alliance of "Mother-God" and "Judy" had decided to kill the "Monster". Somehow, "Mother-God" and "Judy" believed that they could exist after they threw the "Monster" off the Golden Gate Bridge.

There was much talk of suicide and threats of cutting as she went through this stage of treatment, but she didn't act on these self-destructive impulses. On one occasion she went to the Golden Gate Bridge, intent on throwing herself over the railing, but called me from a parking lot at her appointment time and allowed me to coax her back to my office. The old "Mother-God" and "Judy" alliance wanted her dead, but some other aspect of her wanted her to live.

Hospitalisation or increases in medication weren't necessary, however, for Judith not only refused, but seemed to be developing another imaginatively created personality, an internal attitude which was extremely helpful as a counter to the murderous wishes of the harsh punitive superego, "Mother-God". In place of the "Bad Devil", Judith developed the "Smiling Man's Voice", an internal positive superego representation of me which wanted the whole being to live. The "Smiling Man's Voice" aligned with the "Monster" and told the others, as I did, that it was impossible for any aspect of Judith to survive if she tried to kill herself. The "Smiling Man's Voice" told Judith that "Mother-God" and "Judy" could not survive without the "Monster"; furthermore, he reiterated what I had been telling her for weeks, describing how Judith tried to run from herself and responsibility by splitting herself up into different imaginary beings. The "Smiling Man's Voice" and I mimicked each other, reality testing about dissociation, I in external reality and the "Smiling Man's Voice" in internal reality.

Judith's suicidal impulses diminished. She still talked of jumping from the Golden Gate Bridge, but now it was to butt up against a sailboat steered by me. I interpreted this to her as her difficulty with persistent feelings of badness coupled with her desire to be with me, fused with me, as her body in the water floated right next to my boat. I suggested that she wanted to return to the womb.

By her birthday, as we continued to do intensive psychotherapy focused on her unity as one person with widely disparate feelings, wishes and thoughts, "Mother-God" disappeared. Judith had decided to live. Several weeks later, Judith again lay on the floor, writhed around for a while and then was quiet. Then she said: "I've just given birth to a four-and-a-half-year-old girl in a pink checked dress; this time she's dead." Neither "Mother-God" nor "Judy", these two split off aspects of Judith, were necessary at this point.

Dramatic interchanges like this were par for the course with Judith. And of course, things were not black or white: during periods of stress, Judith was prone to regression, with the upsurge of a belief that she was "Judy" dominated by "Mother-God". But for the time being, she saw herself as one person.

The suicidal crisis had passed. There followed a period of some six months of regression. She would spend much of her waking hours in fantasies of nursing and sucking. At first it would be a bottle, then a nipple, then a whole breast. Gradually there were images of penises, penises to suck on, penises to cut off, and penises to bite off. These images were accompanied by great fear and apprehension.

Soon penises were jumping out of my office plants, my shoes and hands. Generally these penises were attacking her mouth. She would abruptly move, as she envisioned an attack by a penis in her reality. Snakes began to attack her in her reality, or sinuously slide through the room or coil in the corner. She began to refer to me as "the rapist", instead of therapist. She had no idea as to what any of this might mean. She had once seen a "pink snake" slithering along the road when she was five years old, while with a relative; she couldn't remember who. With the exception of her little brother, she had never seen a penis as far as she could recall. I wondered why she saw me as "the rapist". She was certain it was fantasy.

The sucking fantasies continued. Some days she would report being filled with a white warm fluid. Other days, she recounted fantasies of being a young girl given enemas and gradually being filled with a whitish fluid. Slowly, recollections of her mother giving her enemas surfaced.

Soon material began to emerge about her grandfather, who had committed suicide shortly before Judith turned six. She had some vague memory of him looking after her after kindergarten. She remembered that in the afternoon her mother would drop her off and grandfather would take her to his workshop. After a few weeks, she recalled that when she was alone in his workshop with him, he asked her if she wanted to be special to him. When she said yes, she wanted to be special to him, he began to molest her; this continued for a year and a half, in various ways.

She revealed this material anxiously, haltingly and in fragments, often convinced that what she was bringing up couldn't be true. She remembered that after every episode he would offer her candy and cookies he kept in a bag. When he offered her sweets, she knew the episode was over and she could relax.

He swore her to secrecy, saying that this was what made her special to him; she complied and kept the secret. She gradually pieced together that she was not only starved for affection and attention, but terrified of him. On a number of occasions he used a gun during the molestations, sexually and threateningly. At other times she reported that he said he would kill himself if she ever told anyone.

Judith had trouble believing these events actually happened, though it all added up. She began vomiting in kindergarten, was taken out of school by her mother and often left in the care of her grandfather. When he committed suicide—with a gun—shortly before she turned six, no one said anything about why he had died. Once again, she blamed herself. She feared she had done something terrible, or thought something terrible, and her grandfather had killed himself because of something she had done or thought or wanted to do or say, to reveal their secret. Needless to say, she said nothing to anyone about it until she told me more than twenty years later.

The previously existing internal split of the "Monster", "Judy" and "Mother-God" worsened, rigidified and solidified as a result of these traumatic events between the ages of four and a half and six. To cope with her grandfather's molestations, the little girl dissociated, removing herself psychologically from the traumatic events. In her four-and-a-half-year-old mind, she wasn't being forced to do sexual things with her grandfather; the "Monster" was engaged in the sexual activities while "Judy" and "Mother-God" stood idly by, observing. When the molestation ended, "Judy" would feed the "Monster" to comfort her, while "Mother-God" would repeat "Such a terrible person" (or the age-appropriate equivalent) over and over again. This intrapsychic scenario served to make her feel even worse, and more confused than she would have from the repeated molestation alone.

Years later, she heard from relatives that her grandfather had been a very bad man. Later still, she heard from another female relative that grandfather had molested her too. But at this time in our work together, Judith was still convinced that it must all be fantasy. Things like this didn't happen in a good family like hers. I told her it was unusual to hallucinate attacking snakes and penises, but the reality of whether or not these events with her grandfather had actually happened had to be deciphered in therapy.

In retrospect, I see that this may have prolonged Judith's confusion. By being neutral and continuing to explore instead of saying it sounded like reality to me, I gave the patient a way out by which she could go along with her usual defences and deny the reality of what had actually happened. In working with this sort of material, I generally listen, aiding the process of material surfacing. Whether this is fantasy or reality, though an important issue, is best left up to the patient to decide at this point. Some patients would rather blame themselves for vile fantasies than look at the possibilities of trauma. Others would rather blame another than accept responsibility for their own fantasies. I wasn't there, so it seems best to let the patient decide and see what defences are being utilised.

It is generally agreed that it is far better for someone to resolve in their own time, as they become increasingly strong psychologically, whether their productions are reality or fantasy. With Judith, such an approach left things open for continued delusional life for several more years, until I stated rather strongly that it seemed very likely to me that she had been sexually traumatised and had great trouble accepting what had happened to her, staying mired in an intermediate world where reality was unclear. To face the fact that her grandfather had molested her would bring up painful feelings from which she could recover. Staying in the intermediate zone, where a very important reality was denied, left her subject to whatever defensive delusions she had created.

During these intervening years, Judith repeatedly slid back into delusions as she tried to stay away from the subject of childhood experience and tried to focus on her reality life, which was going increasingly well both socially and professionally (she had worked continually, from shortly after returning to therapy). But the subject of possible abuse would repeatedly come up as we explored more and more delusional preoccupations and internal splits. Here are some examples of other themes and delusional preoccupations from her treatment.

There were numerous delusions and splits in her internal self-representation which kept from her the knowledge of her own history. For a long time she believed she had her father's child (or perhaps my child) in her uterus. This was in a timeless state, the child was she, was hers and her father's, was ours. The delusion, long held, left only when it was aired and therapeutically resolved.

Believing her own delusional constructs kept her bland on the surface, yet confused and intense internally. She could be convinced of devils, angels, mothers and little girls talking to her with great emotion and force, yet kept it all under wraps. Her intensity had been withdrawn inward; to the outside world, she appeared calm and aloof.

As the origin of her split off selves became clearer, it was possible to focus on a number of dissociated internal beings who were believed in, and at times feared. In addition to "Mother-God" who would punish the "Monster", there were other representations of aspects of her self. There was "Jod I", herself at the age of seven, when difficulties at school manifested themselves. There was "Jod II", a representation of herself at the age of nineteen, haggard and dishevelled while being given shock treatment. Of course, secreted away behind the different selves was the threatening "Grandfather", telling her she was special, and threatening to harm her if she told. Contending for internal space were two others: "Jud", the angry fourteen-year-old, and "Josie", an elderly, incompetent sixty-five-year-old who she feared she would become.

She oscillated among these personae, often associated with binge eating, for "Judy" told her she could eat whatever she wanted and "Mother God" said the calories wouldn't count. To check this out, she could always look in the mirror and see an altered self-image, confirming that she was indeed not gaining weight and years. This grown woman would see a four-and-a-half-year-old child in a pink checked dress in the mirror. Even though this psychological shell game appears tawdry and impossible to us, it was her firm conviction. Whenever her belief was threatened, she would shift from one to another of her personae.

As the various layers of the psychological onion were peeled away, a kernel of personhood emerged as I stated more and more forcefully that I thought it was extremely likely that some traumatic events had occurred. She would protest that it couldn't be so. I asked aloud if I was being "the rapist" with my interpretations.

Gradually, with the usual "two steps forward and one step back" approach, she began gingerly to confront her fear of her grandfather and whatever terrors he had warned her of, should she tell. With this developing awareness of the strong likelihood of molestation, she was able to deal with how furious she was, and grieve for the loss of self and sanity that had persisted for so many years. This integration of intense feeling (anger in this situation) is quintessential; without it, it is extremely likely that the patient is still hiding behind one or another layer of delusional defences. With an acceptance of the full gamut of her own feelings, Judith was on the way to a more healthy approach to life.

Judith has been off antipsychotic medications for more than three decades. It has been a little longer that she has not needed hospitalisation, as she uncovered, explored and worked through a delusional system which had kept her from herself, and hence disorganized and

THE GOOD ANGEL, THE BAD DEVIL 51

confused from childhood on. Having given up her delusional beliefs a number of years ago, she has become much more functional professionally and interpersonally, with only occasional short regressions of several hours or days during periods of stress, which she or I could easily catch. In remembering herself and her history, she has seen that life without the delusional shell game can be possible, pleasurable and rewarding.

Judith had been an "untreatable" schizophrenic, mired in the repetitive cycle of hospitalisations, day care, halfway houses, high antipsychotic drug use and five years of daily hand-holding supportive psychotherapy; she remained lost and "untreatable" until we began our intensive psychotherapy. Was she schizophrenic? Several psychological tests and psychiatrists at three different hospital said she was. I would have no difficulty considering her to have been a case of dissociative disorder, with the dissociative beings projected outside herself. The borderline between schizophrenia and multiple personality disorder has been blurred and changed over the last century (a more thorough explication of this topic is contained in Chapter Seventeen). Is one man's schizophrenia another man's dissociative multiple personality disorder? It's difficult to be sure without the thorough psychotherapeutic exploration afforded by an intensive dynamic psychotherapy.

In any case, childhood trauma has been shown to be instrumental in the development of a certain percentage of people who are diagnosed as schizophrenic. This was the focus of the 2006 national meeting of the US branch of ISPS, The International Society for the Psychological Treatments of Schizophrenia and Other Psychoses, where I presented Judith's case. Most importantly, the childhood traumatic origin of Judith's condition, call it schizophrenia or multiple personality disorder, would never have been elaborated in the typical supportive and heavily medicated treatment which is the usual approach. By giving Judith the chance to engage in an intensive psychotherapy, she has achieved wholeness and cure (off antipsychotic medication for more than thirty years), when the best achieved with her previous five years of care was the status of an "untreatable" schizophrenic who needed constant attention and ineffective (and very expensive) supportive care.

The options are as follows: "untreatable" schizophrenic, heavily medicated and in constant supportive care, requiring five years of repeated hospitalisations, day care and daily individual and group therapy, versus an intensive psychotherapy which led over the course of several years to integration, healing and cure, free of all antipsychotic medication for more than thirty years. Judith tells me that she prefers the latter: she prefers the cure to her previously "untreatable" schizophrenic state.

CHAPTER EIGHT

The pugilist, Mary, and the mother with the fiery halo

When I first saw Daphne nearly thirty years ago, she was a brown haired woman in her mid-fifties. She was in the hospital for perhaps the thirty-fifth time in her life. Her psychiatrist of twenty years was retiring and transferring her to my care. She was alternately withdrawn or bellicose, and had been thrown out of several hospitals for her boxing skills, as she would physically attack other patients or staff.

She was an attractive married woman, a mother of two, who had made a number of suicide attempts over the previous thirty years. At one point she had jumped from the Golden Gate Bridge but had (seemingly miraculously) fallen on the catwalk below, broken many bones, and spent a number of months in the hospital recovering physically, if not psychologically. She had worked at several jobs, but had always lost them due to actions viewed as bizarre and idiosyncratic, for example writing strange notes in the margins of memos and verbally attacking her superiors.

Her history, as given by Daphne, her husband, and the referring psychiatrist, revealed periods of pressured, manic-seeming behaviour, accompanied by or alternating with profound and severe depression.

She was diagnostically considered to be schizoaffective or somewhere on the bipolar spectrum of manic-depressive disorder, but couldn't be contained by the antipsychotic, antidepressant and mood stabilising medicines then available, including lithium. There was also the question of a schizophrenic quality, because she seemed so disturbed and strange at times, hallucinating and talking to herself.

In my first interview with Daphne, it was clear that she was distracted, both physically and psychologically. She often looked beyond me, through me or over me. I asked the obvious question: "What are you staring at?" She didn't answer straight away, but did say that she was surprised I had asked; her previous psychiatrists hadn't. I immediately had the sense that she had some hallucinatory reality to which she went if pressured; perhaps she lived in an unseen inner world. I expected that she would volunteer nothing to me about it, even as to whether or not such a delusional reality existed. I noted it, and from time to time over the first few months of treatment would say something like this: "You seem to be looking at and perhaps communicating with something that you see and I don't; care to tell me about it?"

I was not surprised by her lack of response, since I was simply trying to establish an inquiring beachhead by stating the obvious in an attempt to get Daphne to start observing herself. I hoped that my telling her that she seemed immersed in an inner world might gradually lead to her telling me the contents of this inner world, if one actually existed. After all, if I was open to the possibility that in her mind there were more than just the two of us in the room, perhaps she could begin to disclose her internal preoccupations to me. Several months later, during a family interview with Daphne's husband and one of her children, both said they had noticed such behaviour for years. According to the child, who was by this time an adult, Mom often looked like she was talking to someone, and had done so for as long as the child could remember.

Delusional people, like the rest of us, are often ambivalent. Daphne was no exception. She wanted to keep her delusional world her secret, but she also wanted to talk about it, to tell it to someone. Since it was so important to her, she wanted to share it with another person in the hope of validation and corroboration. She kind of knew it was strange, so had only once told anyone anything about it. The results were unsettling, so she had continued to keep it her secret.

As she would later tell me, she revealed to her previous psychiatrist that she had a friend named "Mary" and he had asked her to express "Mary". Daphne did, and proceeded to pummel him. They were both so shaken by this experience that they left "Mary" alone thereafter: he because he felt that "Mary" was more than either of them could handle; she because she didn't want to hurt her beloved psychiatrist again. He probably should have inquired more about "Mary" rather than just try to have Daphne express "Mary" as she did. Expressing the contents of an internal being puts the patient fully into the character of the internal being, as happened to Daphne when she expressed "Mary". It is much more dangerous to ask the patient to express the inner being rather than to ask the patient abut the inner creation and gradually get a little distance from it. Once having let "Mary" out in such a way, the therapist should have pursued the course of taking a history of how "Mary" developed, why she was so angry, and what her life was like.

At this point we had been working together for several months, now twice a week in my office. Daphne was no longer in the hospital; her family tried to look after her at home. She continued to look off in space; I continued to make comments about her seeming preoccupied and distracted, and wondered out loud what or who she was looking at. One day, in response to these observations, she said she was talking with "Mary". Who was "Mary", I asked. "Mary" was her friend. How long had she known "Mary"? "Oh, since I was three." This was just what I was waiting for. I quickly began to take a history of the origin of the delusional being, "Mary".

The following history of "Mary" was gleaned from Daphne and from "Mary". Obviously it came only from Daphne, but it is strategic to treat an emerging delusional personality as if it were an existing entity. It is a simple enough thing to do: merely inquire about the imaginary person and his or her life history, habits and relationships. When I treat this imaginary being as if it were a real person, the patient—the only one who is really talking to me—does not feel affronted and brings up material that might otherwise go underground.

When Daphne was a year and a half old, her mother gave birth to another daughter. Daphne's mother was very "mean", depressed, and withdrawn much of the time, and seemed to Daphne to squander what little positive energy she had on her newborn. Daphne became jealous of her younger sister, and by the age of two and a half she hated her. She remembers being on the front porch with her sister in a baby carriage. All of a sudden an older girl appeared above Daphne's head, and told her to push the baby carriage off the porch. This older girl would eventually be named "Mary".

Daphne was ambivalent, both hating and loving her younger sister. She solved her dilemma by doing both: she pushed the baby carriage off the porch while holding on to it, with the result that she and baby sister went screaming, crying and crashing down the hill. "Mary", inexplicably, flew over them both, laughing away. Daphne was punished severely by her mother, and not for the first time. By her account, her mother would often keep her in a closet for days, with little food, water or sanitation, sometimes beating her. During these times, "Mary", still un-named, would regale Daphne with stories, or get Daphne to laugh at her mother, which only drove the mother into even more sadistic behaviour.

Daphne's internal maelstrom only worsened when her abusive, alcoholic father began to molest her when she was four. To try to cope with these molestations, Daphne would go off and play with her friend in the air while her father heaved away on the bed. That was when a new being emerged, "the girl". It was "the girl" who cried and sobbed and took both parents' abuse, while Daphne and her friend (soon to be known as "Mary") would gleefully play in the air, looking down at the painful things happening to "the girl". Sexual abuse by her father continued for a number of years. Daphne was unable to mobilise herself to deal with her father's abuse because of her fear of him. Instead, she would dissociate from "the girl" to whom things were happening, and immerse herself in a joyful life with "Mary".

"Mary" took on a name when Daphne was five. Daphne and an actual friend named Mary were playing with matches and started a fire, which burned and consumed much of the town she lived in. Her parents used this as further proof of Daphne's badness and forbade her ever again playing with her real friend Mary. No real loss to Daphne; she simply gave her imaginary friend the name of her banished friend Mary.

Like her lost friend, "Mary" had blonde hair and blue eyes, while Daphne was brown haired with hazel eyes. "Mary" was always a year or two older than Daphne, until she ("Mary") reached eighteen;

at this point "Mary" stopped aging. Within two years, Daphne caught up in age with "Mary". Even though Daphne was in her fifties when I first met her, "Mary" was still eighteen. Together, the two of them did a lot of zany, energetic and giddy teenage things.

"Mary" was very assertive; Daphne felt that she was not. What looked like the interaction of polarities—sometimes enthusiastic, sometimes depressed—was in fact immersion in (and acting out of) the delusion of "Mary". For example, Daphne became an excellent tennis player,but it was not only Daphne playing; in her mind it was she and "Mary" playing. When she would rush the net, or serve with great force, it was always "Mary's" energy and vitality that carried the day and helped Daphne win.

Daphne had been isolated and lived in a world apart. She had married, but her husband knew nothing of her mind's inner workings. Just as Daphne wanted a friend and had "Mary", "Mary" wanted to talk, to tell me about her life and their life together. To questions posed to Daphne, such as "What was it like for 'Mary'?" or "What were you doing when Daphne did such and such?" "Mary" gradually and proudly confided in me. "Mary" told me during a number of sessions what she had done in her life. When she would write those bizarre comments in the margins of office memos, it was because Daphne and "Mary" were playing, and having so much fun. When Daphne left her own small children unattended—sometimes for hours—while she went into a closet, it was to relive her own experience with her mother and be regaled by "Mary" with whatever playful internally boisterous invention was being created. When Daphne jumped from the Golden Gate Bridge, it was just a lark, impelled by "Mary"; she only landed on the catwalk because Daphne didn't want to die and made sure she hit something solid. In effect, Daphne was both in and out of a delusional state, enough to keep her alive, but not enough to protect herself from her erstwhile friend's playful and deadly games.

This series of tales and events of "Mary" was developed in a number of threads over the first year of therapy. It was not one clear-cut exposition of the history of a delusional state. Time was spent talking about Daphne's day-to-day life as well. Of course her depressions and suicidal urges had to be dealt with too, and for this, occasional family meetings were held to stabilise Daphne and provide whatever protection was necessary.

Gradually, interspersed with details of Daphne's life and their joint history of "Mary" (for both of them were willing to give me information), more material emerged about other delusional figures in Daphne's internal life. This new information emerged slowly and fitfully as I asked questions about whether or not anything else might exist on a similar level as "Mary". Illusory as these beings appear to us, Daphne believed they existed as much as "Mary", herself and me. There was the threatening "man", representing her father, and the angry, critical fiery "woman whose head was ringed with flames", representing her mother. They had both been with her from the age of four or five. She didn't know if "Mary" came before them; they had all been there for so long. When Daphne couldn't escape her fear of both her critical internalised mother and her angry, threatening internalised father, she left "the girl" to deal with both of them while she and "Mary" went off to play.

Suicide attempts and hospitalisations were caused by this dissociative mind play. In the mind of Daphne during more than fifty years, things became very complicated. At times "the girl" would make a suicide attempt because she felt so terrible, or to escape one of her internal parental tormentors. Even though it was Daphne who made the suicide attempt, in her mind it was the miserable "girl" who tried to kill herself, while Daphne, playing with "Mary", rattled around in some externalised space, unable and unwilling to help "the girl" who was really Daphne. Sometimes Daphne and "Mary" would follow "Mary's" suggestion and goad "the girl" into some self-destructive behaviour, leading to hospitalisation. At other times, Daphne (with "Mary") would act so bizarrely and antagonistically that she would be hospitalised for overt psychosis or threatening behaviour.

T. S. Eliot's line "In my beginning is my end" applies to the analysis and exploration of delusional beings. In the telling, in the historical review of how the delusion forms, a slight interjection of rationality begins. But it is a struggle for soul and life, and "Mary" was not going to go easily. For so many years, while believing she was playing with "Mary", Daphne had acted in such self-destructive ways that I anticipated there would be suicidal crises; and so there were. For a period of a little less than a year, Daphne remained suicidal. To give up a best friend is difficult, never mind a best friend to whom one is fused in an even more compelling internal delusional reality. To give up a best friend who appeared to have saved one from the terrors inflicted on "the girl" would be even more difficult. To be left as the vulnerable "girl", which is what Daphne feared she would become without "Mary", was even more frightening.

I stayed as attuned as possible to the likelihood of suicide, taking all threats quite seriously and hospitalising Daphne for four reasonably short periods as she gave up her delusional world of "Mary". Usually the hospitalisation itself was enough, but once she secreted a lethal dose of pills in her vagina, and took a serious overdose in the hospital at "Mary's" direction. She survived because she was on a closely supervised suicide watch, and only had the pills in her system for a short time.

This suicide attempt was "Mary's" last gasp. Daphne finally realised how serious this mind game of hers was, and began to use her own intellect to protect herself against going off with "Mary". She saw how she loved being with "Mary", how any sadness or anxiety would lead to her going off to her delusional reality, leaving the undefended, vulnerable "girl" to handle situations that were difficult externally and overwhelming internally. Little by little over the next few months, some of it in the hospital, she relinquished a delusional system that had lasted fifty-five years.

Of course the psychotherapy and her relationship with me were pivotal in unearthing Daphne's delusional and dissociative way of being. Daphne's relationship to me was crucial in this uncovering and healing process. But the relationship alone was not enough; after all she had had an extremely strong and good relationship with her previous analyst of more than twenty years. What was required with Daphne was a combination of a good working alliance between the two of us and the necessity for us to look at and understand her dissociative and delusional productions through an intensive, inquiring psychotherapy. Firstly, she had to recognise the existence of an alternative reality in which she lived much of the time. Then, when she acknowledged that she left painful external reality for a seemingly more comfortable internal reality, we could focus on the internal delusional reality and gradually lead her back to the consensually agreed world in which we all live most of the time.

Through this intensive psychotherapeutic approach, Daphne healed. She returned to work, had ten good years with her husband before his death, and was reconciled with her children. Some family sessions aided in the transition to a good family life; all her family needed to know was that it really wasn't intentional on her part and that she had been terribly confused for all those years. She continues to lead an active life with many friends. "Mary" is hardly ever necessary.

Years later, when I told her previous, much loved psychiatrist, about Daphne's successful treatment, he was chagrined that he had not pursued his ample psychoanalytic understanding and taken a more thorough history of "Mary". Though very well trained at one of the premier long term psychiatric hospitals in the country, he—like so many in our field—had operated with the assumption that one had to treat severely disturbed patients with kid gloves, not with an intensive psychodynamic psychotherapy. Such a supportive approach never got to the heart of Daphne's difficulties.

Daphne is now aware of whatever she does to bring up "Mary". If stressed or overwhelmed by real life experiences, she is aware that she might go off to "Mary". She is forewarned, and hence armed with her own rational perspective to understand "Mary" and the destructive aspects of delusional life. For the last twenty-five years, she has been essentially delusion-free.

CHAPTER NINE

Two rats and the extraterrestrial

ois was a depressed, withdrawn woman in her mid-thirties
when she consulted me. She had a previous diagnosis of
chronic paranoid schizophrenia, had been hospitalised several
times, and had been treated for the previous seven years with antipsychotic medication. She had lived in a halfway house for the better part
of a year and now stayed alone in a rooming house. She was unkempt,
dishevelled, and clearly preoccupied and hallucinating. She had been
married, but was now divorced. She had given up custody of her
children, and had had a persistent delusion for years that two rats
were gnawing away at her. She had little contact with anyone except
for an old friend of hers who sent her to me. By everyone's account
(previous friends, family, psychiatrists and ancillary staff), she was a
hopeless case.

The diagnosis of chronic schizophrenia had been made during
one of her first hospitalisations, when she told a psychiatrist about
the two rats gnawing at her. The diagnosis was more correct than he
knew, but by failing to help her try to fathom the meaning of the two
rats gnawing at her, he missed the opportunity to open a pathway to
an understanding of Lois' projected imagination.

People with delusions are beset by images and a concatenation
of feelings that are impossible for them to bear, or at least to bear

in their current vulnerable state. Hence the delusion, the projection outside themselves of issues they can't handle. Like Freud's notion of the return of the repressed, having to do with issues one has put out of consciousness coming back to bedevil one, these people—due perhaps to a greater imaginative quality, perhaps to a poorer synthetic ability, perhaps to more pain and trauma in life—project issues outside themselves. But the projected issues, like a tethered rubber ball on a paddle, keep coming back to where they began. The fearful, isolated, lonely paranoid gets the interest and involvement he or she craves, but to a much more heightened and intense extent than anyone could ever desire. In the delusion or hallucination, though, may lie a key to the code of the person's thinking. Sometimes, as the two previous cases illustrate, it may take years to decipher the meaning of delusions; here it was much simpler.

The opening lay in the two rats gnawing at Lois. "Do two rats gnawing at you mean anything to you?" I asked. Needless to say, she hadn't been asked that question by previous psychiatrists or even thought very much about the meaning of such a powerful image. As usual, since this was early in my years of treating people, I was dumbfounded that she hadn't been asked about the meaning of her image; unfortunately, though, I was beginning to expect such a reply. What this said about our profession and the way most of us treat schizophrenics and delusional people, I was only beginning to suspect.

I always find it strange that a person can be totally immersed in a terrifying or otherwise very upsetting series of thoughts or a delusion, and not think much about why they're having such thoughts, nor be asked by their psychiatrist what the meaning of such thoughts is to them. How can one gain control over psychotic material if one can't step back and understand it? How can patient or psychiatrist make sense of bizarre delusions if they never discuss their possible content and meaning?

What did the two rats mean? She didn't know. I had some sense immediately, for she had two children. When did the image begin? It was during the long (six-month) hospitalisation after the birth of her younger child, when she couldn't bear to see her children, and felt terribly guilty about being away from them, yet unable to handle any interaction with them. I asked: "Could the two rats burrowing into your heart symbolize anything, perhaps your two children entering your heart? Perhaps the two rats represent your loving and missing them." She hadn't thought about such a possibility.

This not having thought about it is a major part of the difficulty in a delusional person. If they did think about it, the meaning would most likely become clear, as did the meaning of the two rats. But the issues involved are, for whatever idiosyncratic reason, too much. Such a person needs help to understand the meaning of his or her productions, the psychological mechanisms involved, and most of all, to deal with the underlying feelings that led to the formation of delusions. This is why it is essential that the treating psychiatrist or therapist attempt to help clarify the ramifications of illusions, delusions and hallucinations. If he does not, but merely diagnoses and medicates, this often leaves a patient without a channel to understanding him- or herself.

She agreed that the rats might represent her two children gnawing at her feelings. She seemed comforted by this sense, and much more willing to bring up historical and (gradually, over a period of several months of twice weekly psychotherapy) intrapsychic and emotional material that had persisted for many years.

She was the only child of a critical and negative mother and a loving, indulgent father. Her father loved her unconditionally and served as a buffer against the constant jibes and denigrating comments of her mother. Her mother excoriated her; her father extolled her. When she was seven, Lois and her father were told by her intimidating, extremely impressive old Russian ballet teacher that she "dances like she comes from another planet".

This served as the seed of a delusion, a delusion from those early years of life that she came from outer space. If she did come from outer space, this might account for her mother's criticism and caustic comments. She was sheltered in her father's love, because he too must come from outer space; her mother must be an Earthling, jealous of her extraterrestrial origin. Such a belief comforted her, seeming innocuous enough, but it was laden with unforeseen difficulty.

When she was thirteen, her father died unexpectedly. She was grief-stricken and had to be hospitalised for a number of months. During those months she did what might be expected for someone who has broken the bounds of reality. She created a further delusion, this time of her father always with her. She had never talked of this to anyone before, neither when hospitalised in her early teens nor during later hospitalisations and other periods of psychotherapy. She felt safe enough to tell me this, perhaps because she had been so frightened of the two rats which we had deciphered, perhaps because she felt we could both speak the same language, the language of understanding the meaning of her delusional imagery.

Since his death more than twenty years previously, her father had been by her side all her waking life. When she passed someone a cup of coffee, she passed him one too. When she went cycling, he went along on his own bike. Whatever she did, she was accompanied by her much loved father. He was kept healthy and whole in her delusional reality: as far as Lois was concerned, her father remained vibrant and alive, not mouldering and decaying in the ground. Long days and nights, when she was apparently alone, were spent immersed in conversation and delight with her lost and protective father.

She kept her delusion a secret, probably because some part of her knew her father was dead and she didn't want to disrupt her internal world with the harsh world of a reality that included her continuously sniping (and now depressed) mother and the fact that her father had died. She appeared to the world to be recovered from the serious decompensation that had led to her adolescent hospitalisation, but internally she maintained a rich and vivid delusional life and constant activities with her father.

Externally, Lois appeared to keep it together enough so that she married in her late teens. In her early twenties, she went further into her comforting delusions of her father when her first husband hanged himself for no apparent reason other than that he was having a "bad trip" on the psychedelic drugs he was taking at the time. Another sudden and unexpected death reinforced her retreat into delusional reality. Several years later she married a very understanding, solid man who looked after her until she decompensated in the postpartum period after the birth of their second child.

A delusional reality is both fragile and rigid. Patients cling to delusions tenaciously, and having once created delusions, have the propensity to become delusional in every possible way. Lois had two very important losses which she attempted to deal with by creating the delusional reality of her comforting father. Now, with her breakdown in her thirties, she developed paranoid delusions that terrified her, in addition to the delusion of the rats gnawing away at her heart.

Once delusional, one is always vulnerable to delusional crises and regressions, until the delusions and the mechanisms of delusion formation are explored and understood. Once one has fractured the bounds of reality, for whatever reason, one is prone to increasing delusion formation.

What harm is there in the protective delusion of the father to help an adolescent cope with his death? The harm lies in the increasing propensity to develop all types of delusions, running the gamut from protective to playful to destructive and terrorising. In the process, one's actual self is buried under a layer of self-obfuscating phenomena contained within the delusion.

In the telling of her delusions and history, with a little prodding from me about how difficult it was to accept her father's death, her mother's neglect and abusiveness, and the other pains of life, Lois gave up her delusions. She recognised that the belief that she was an extraterrestrial was a way of seeming important and special, as she had seemed special to her ballet teacher and definitely was special to her father. It was a way to protect her from her mother and give importance to her existence.

The delusion of her father constantly with her evaporated over a period of about three months, aided by a few hospitalisations of several days to keep her from harming herself. To give up this delusion was risky. Not only was it comforting, but she had never mourned her father's death twenty years earlier. In addition, the fused, psychotic delusional intensity meant that, if anything, her father meant more to her as a delusional object (figure) than as a real and loving person.

My experience with delusional people is that they are very creative. Consequently, I wasn't surprised when Lois found an extremely imaginative means to give up the long held delusion of her father. This relinquishing of the delusion of her father was accomplished by the development of a transitional, short-term delusion of her two children constantly by her side. In short, she substituted her children for her father in delusion-land. (Once open to delusion formation, there is no end to them, until one becomes aware of what one is doing.) Rather than being an impediment, though, this new delusion was a flash of inspiration and a therapeutic aid. We were able to talk about her yearning for those she loved, whether father or estranged children. She used delusions as a way of believing she was in contact with loved ones, all the while feeling powerless to actually be in contact with them. Delusions were seen as her yearning for those she loved.

With this change of focus towards the world, and an emphasis on the means of reconciling with her children—a definite possibility, as opposed to being in touch with her long dead father—Lois gave up all delusions and focused all her energy on her children. Without internal delusions taking up her loving vital energy, she was able to contact her former husband and re-establish a very good and continuing relationship with her children. In addition, she became quite successful at two different careers, neither of which was ballet.

Her twenty-year-long delusional orientation dissolved over a six- to eight-month period. We had talked her language in such a way that her psychic energy could travel outwards towards life, instead of incessantly cycling inwardly towards delusion, blockage and death. She finished therapy, having achieved more gains than she had ever dared to hope for. Over some years she kept in touch by mail, apparently having maintained the gains of an exploratory psychotherapy of delusions without resort to dramatic and delusional representations of feeling states.

Lois, a previously "untreatable" paranoid schizophrenic viewed as a heavily medicated, burnt out case, remained off medication. Through an intensive exploratory psychotherapy, she had understood her own symbolism. Instead of a terrified, haggard, overly medicated schizophrenic afraid of her own hallucinations, she has been cured. She had become an independent person, off antipsychotic medication, with meaningful relationships, work, and access to the meaning of her own imaginative creations.

CHAPTER TEN

The ghost in the history

The following is a shorter vignette, spread over nearly two years, perhaps fifty sessions in all. It will be clear that the intensity of the material is far less compelling than in some of the other cases, yet still demonstrates that even a short, infrequent, insight-oriented psychotherapy such as this one may have profound healing and curative effects. The reader will also notice, as I did during the course of this treatment, that the emerging psychological material is at a distance, serving an intellectualising defensive function for the patient. The reasons for this may be many. Dealing with another man and one's attendant fears may entail enlisting certain intellectual defences, rooted in anxiety. A short-term, less intensive therapy such as this one may be due to the patient's adjusting the frequency of visits, thereby limiting them to what he thinks he can handle.

Paranoid defences are intellectual ways of binding anxiety through leaping to conclusions, just as distancing from the therapist and the feared, potentially overwhelming intrapsychic and emotional material is another intellectual way to remove oneself from anxiety. Since the diagnosis here was paranoia, the hysterical and highly emotional defences seen in some of the other cases do not apply.

At times, the truly paranoid person can seem like an old Western hero: calm, cool, collected and totally delusional. The calmness is the defence against overwhelming fear; the coolness is in the service of removing himself from his terror. Unfortunately, the collected appearance of such people is a cover for intense fear, in the service of premises and conclusions that do not bear any rational scrutiny.

Roger was a professional man, single and isolated. He had immigrated a little more than three years earlier and missed his far-flung family and friends. Even though he was quite successful at work, he had become increasingly apprehensive about any social interaction, certain that messages were being sent to him in many ways and from multiple sources.

This was very troubling, for he had no idea what he was supposed to do with these less than obvious communications. He knew he wasn't a communist, but sometimes people wore red, hence they were calling him a communist. Was he supposed to hug or kiss the women in the cafeteria queue who appeared to be giving him come-on signals by moving one hand or the other, or gesturing in a way that (to him) had much sexual innuendo? What was he supposed to do with green at the corner traffic light, a colour which he was certain referred to money and his greed?

He was in agony about the messages he believed were being sent to him. It didn't occur to him that he was the one constant in many situations, and that he was misinterpreting reality and relating nearly everything to himself. He felt certain that others were responsible for the inferences he drew, inferences that he viewed not as inferences, but as reality.

He jumped from conclusion to conclusion as to the people who might be tormenting him. Increasingly he had difficulty at work, for he was certain that a plot had developed to embarrass him. Gradually the plot took on more concrete form, as he became convinced that he was the object of a plan to frame him for a kickback scheme. Diverse phenomena became facts indicating the existence of such a framing scheme. The company name on the water fountain, the type of paper or software being used, and the gestures of his colleagues all demonstrated that he was not long for this job. Not only was he not long for the job, but he was certain that prison and deportation awaited him.

Roger was in a state of intense anxiety about the effects of the plot to frame him. He misinterpreted any type of gesture. As with all people with paranoid delusions, he was unfortunately convinced that he perceived them correctly. He had always been considered smart and didn't doubt the reality of his perceptions. Convinced that he was correct in all that he perceived, Roger vigilantly attempted to ward off the anticipated consequences that he feared would ensue.

In his country of origin, people rarely came for psychiatric help. For him to follow the advice of colleagues at work (who sensed the anxiety and isolation he exuded) and seek psychiatric help meant that he was suffering terribly. He couldn't sleep at night, was constantly startled, inappropriate in his responses (understandably, since he was filtering every stimulus and interaction through his certainty that he was being framed), and obviously anxious.

Roger thought about killing those responsible for his plight, but didn't know who they were. He thought about killing himself, but he hadn't done anything wrong and his relatives in the "old country" depended on him. He just wanted to get to the bottom of the framing scheme, report the framers and have them punished. Could I help him with this?

People who are relatively naive and untutored psychologically may be much more able to benefit from psychiatric intervention than those who have become culturally and personally acclimatised to notions like paranoia. Roger invested me with great powers as the healer, shaman or medicine man. Yet because of his cultural orientation, it was unlikely that he would stay for a serious and prolonged psychotherapy of his delusional system. He was only seeing me out of desperation. How best to enter in and help? As usual, I took a history.

Roger was the fourth child of seven, the second eldest boy. He was the first in his family to go to the equivalent of college and professional school. There was much external and internal pressure on him to succeed. He sent a good portion of his handsome salary back to his family. In short, he was a good and dutiful son.

Had he ever had anything like this happen before? Never. It just started when he came to this country. This was a way in. He was obviously very bright; he might accept a simple formulation like: perhaps you're lonely here, miss people, and are somehow misinterpreting stimuli because you are so lonely. I figured I'd give it a try. "Perhaps, coming from a culture and family in which there was so much personal involvement with you, you are seeking contact with people through your belief that people are sending you messages.

It's always difficult in a new country, and it takes time to meet new people. Maybe the idea that people are sending you messages has to do with your feeling lonely and wishing people were involved with you." He didn't think this was so, but would consider it.

This last half denial, half tentative agreement was about the best that could be expected. Even though I knew his troubles were much deeper and more serious, the "inexact interpretation" regarding loneliness and relating stimuli to himself served the purpose of giving him some schema, some fabric that was far less troubling than the notion of a vague conspiracy against him. With this explanation he could perhaps start to decipher his troubles.

I also gave him some antipsychotic medication, but he quickly stopped it due both to side effects and to his sense that there really was nothing wrong with him, so why take medicines. He was improving somewhat, perhaps due to ventilating his anxieties and becoming less isolated as he talked to me, or perhaps due to the inexact interpretation. The plots continued, but were less distressing.

We now began to talk more about his history. What was childhood like? As we talked of the environment in which he grew up, replete with doting relatives, he mentioned that his father had been away for three years during his early childhood. He had gone to another country to better himself financially, and just as Roger did, he sent money back home. Unfortunately, his father had been framed by his colleagues at work and was sent home in disgrace. This had been a tragedy to him and to the extended family.

Even though the parallels were obvious to the listener, they were not to the patient. Over a number of sessions of once weekly psychotherapy, the similarities became clearer. Roger was an immigrant, just like his father. His father had survived in a foreign country for only three years; Roger had been in this country for a little more than three years. Unconsciously, time pressures were building in him around the three-year survival time in a foreign country. His father had been framed; Roger saw plots to frame him in every corner. Roger feared that he, like his father, would be framed. Family honour was extremely important too; he feared that he too, like his father, would be sent home in disgrace.

Here another thread could be tied together. Roger was lonely. He really didn't like his life in this country, without festivals, family involvement and a multitude of friends. Could it be that contrary to his conscious desire to stay in this country as a hero and benefactor to his family, he was unconsciously trying to get himself sent back to a place where people cared about him, just as his father had been sent back? He didn't think so, but would consider these threads and possibilities as well.

As Roger cleared, another theme emerged from his early history: the blaming, critical attitude of his immediate and extended family. Someone was always at fault. Those who framed his father were guilty; even his father was responsible for not having been smart enough to sense the schemes and plots going on around him in the foreign land.

Roger, too, had been blamed and shamed from his earliest days; this was the primary mode used in his family for educating children. In addition, he was often threatened with the punishment of being put in the dumb waiter, where the family ghost lived. He never was actually put in the dumb waiter, but he was threatened with it. Roger was raised to believe that ghosts and evil spirits inhabited the dumb waiter and caused destructive events to happen in life.

The family believed that evil spirits, sent by people jealous of his father's success, had caused his father to be framed. Spirits, both good and bad, were possible in the pantheon of his culture. Spirits existed in the dumb waiter of his own house, and were used as a threat to keep him and the other children in line. In a country of animistic and pantheistic belief, the evil eye was a definite possibility and could apply even in San Francisco. Perhaps someone in his country of origin was envious of him and his success; perhaps that was the cause of the ubiquitous plotting against him.

These themes and subtexts, although obvious to the reader, required some time to be worked through and resolved. Roger's anxiety and constant sense of being besieged gradually diminished over the course of two years. His paranoia dissolved to the point where he became involved with a woman, got married and settled down. He became less anxious at work, and his intelligence and abilities led to a number of promotions.

Over the two-year period of insight-oriented psychotherapy, this very delusional man cleared enough that he could begin to live his own life, less fettered by the ghosts of his past and his ongoing transference beliefs and fears. Since it was such a short course of treatment, he may regress under some future stressor, but he has shown both psychological resilience and the ability to integrate concepts that were totally alien to him, with extremely beneficial effects.

Even though I felt there was a great deal more to the story, we must accept that this was as far as Roger was willing to go at that time. The material is consequently filtered and shaded under the diffusing arc of rationality and intellectual defences and thought. Though not a dramatic therapy compared to the storms and crises of some of the others, it served the purpose of helping this very delusional man get some distance from the ghosts and demons of paranoia which possessed him.

If the results of this therapy last, who can say it needed to be conducted on a deeper level; if the results don't last, he can always seek additional psychotherapy to truly understand the projection of his fears and conflicts onto others and accept his anxieties and tender feelings as his own.

CHAPTER ELEVEN

Stalemate

The following psychotherapy, like the previous one, is a highly intellectualised, removed and less emotional one. The very nature of paranoia is that it is a projection onto others and a denial of responsibility for one's own feelings and underlying psychological issues. The material seems to the paranoid person to be coming from outside himself and to have little to do with him. Paranoid people have the logical concept of inference mixed up with the notion of implication. They think others are implying, whereas the paranoid person is really inferring.

Such was the situation in the following clinical example. In the process of trying to get away from his difficulties, the patient, Peter, toned down the underlying emotions and conflicts. Our sense of him is dimmer, in part because the diminishing of intensity is part of the mechanism of paranoia: the intent is to isolate and remove feelings that are sensed to be overwhelming. For various reasons it is too painful to feel one's feelings, so one invents fantastical stories for oneself to assuage one's hurt, isolation, resentment and need for another person.

Here too, the frequency of psychotherapy was titrated down by the patient. This is an attempt to protect him from himself and to try and help him remove himself from me, just as the paranoia removes him from real relationships. Even such a watered-down psychotherapy of a delusional patient, however, may have substantive and beneficial effects.

Occasionally a markedly delusional patient comes along who is both so intelligent and so intractably paranoid that the best that can be hoped for in the course of a short-term psychotherapy is a type of therapeutic impasse, where the patient saves face and insists on the correctness of his paranoid beliefs, while clinical improvement occurs. Such a stalemate is unsatisfying for the therapist, but may be of crucial help to the patient in terms of work, relationships and involvement in life.

Peter was brilliant in a field well known for eccentric and highly idiosyncratic thought and behaviour. He was so disturbed, however, that he came to the attention of family and colleagues, and was eventually referred to me with the admonition that I should try to put him on a long-lasting antipsychotic medicine. I tried, but patients' rights being what they were and are, it was impossible to keep him on either oral or intramuscular medication. During the short time he was taking antipsychotics, there appeared to be no change in his floridly paranoid orientation and behaviour.

Peter was a lonely, isolated young man in his late twenties, and had a far-flung delusional system revolving around Harold Geneen, the former president of ITT (International Telephone & Telegraph). This delusional system had persisted for four years and worsened perniciously as he invented more and more permutations to his belief system. For him it wasn't a belief system, it was reality. He was such a precociously smart fellow that he mired himself more and more deeply into a morass of his own creation.

Peter was the eldest of four, a highly intelligent child who was felt to be a genius, and repeatedly demonstrated his brilliance throughout school. A brother two years younger and two younger sisters were less gifted and had a far easier time adjusting to the world. His recollections of his parents were that they were each accomplished in their own right, valuing scholastic achievement and the work ethic. There was some physical closeness with his mother during his first few years, but little playfulness in childhood. His father was seen as an authoritarian, controlling and high-minded man with little time for his children. Peter grew up a lonely, isolated young man, with

few friends and an interest in solitary athletics and academic achievement. He didn't date much and was unaccustomed to women. Most
of his energy was poured into his academic programme, where he
was esteemed for his abilities.

Then Peter met Jeanine while he was bike riding. He and she rode
for about an hour together. He asked for her phone number; she gave
him one. It was the wrong number. He tried as many permutations
as were possible of the number, but to no avail. She had given him a
fictitious number. He was devastated. Here was the first woman he
was interested in, and she deceived him. But had she really deceived
him? There was a spark between them; he knew that she had really
liked him. Perhaps she was being prevented from seeing him, hence
the wrong telephone number. It was clear to Peter that she had
wanted to see him again; someone powerful and controlling must
have intervened and changed the number she had given him.

Suddenly he knew that Harold Geneen had changed her phone
number. Since he headed a large phone company (it being international didn't make any difference) only he would have the power to
change the number. Harold Geneen must be her father (didn't they
have a name in common?) interfering and trying to keep his daughter
from Peter. Of course the spelling of Geneen and Jeanine being different didn't count; he had always been sure of his conclusions, and
didn't realise that he was now entering a delusional quagmire.

Peter quickly descended into a paranoid system that included
phones being tapped, people not being who they said they were,
secret agents, and thoughts being read. Highly developed machines
read his thoughts and transmitted them to the higher-ups at ITT; his
every action was monitored, as was his behaviour. His intelligence
did him a disservice. He was able to read any interaction as the revelation of this underground plot to keep him from his beloved. He
was so certain that she must be trying to make contact with him that
he read messages into newspapers, television ads and passing cars;
all were trying to tell him that she was really interested in him but
was being kept from him by the all-powerful father.

By the time he came to see me, he was in a quandary. Whom
should he turn to? The police and FBI were under the control of
Harold Geneen, for it was well known that he had espionage and
CIA connections. Peter was thinking of taking some kind of action
to free her from the essential house arrest which he knew kept her at

home, imprisoned and unable to see him, but he had no idea where to begin. Family and colleagues, who had seen him deteriorate, could only suggest psychiatric care. He was absolutely convinced of the clarity of his perceptions and position. He spent a year in once to twice weekly psychotherapy, with one short hospitalisation. During that time, I made attempts to use antipsychotics in the hope of diminishing the anxiety he wasn't even aware he felt, but he would have little of it.

Our time was spent in several fashions. Understanding Peter's situation and getting as clear a picture as possible of the difficulties he was in were the first order of the day. I tried to empathise as much as possible with how upset and lonely he was. I sympathised with the difficulty of this situation for him, made it clear that I saw it somewhat differently, and suggested we try to see if there could be any psychological and emotional reasons for his convictions. Up to this point he had responded cordially. But when I raised the possibility that his perceptions might be rooted in loneliness and loss, that the malign plot might be his way of telling himself that Jeanine was really interested in him when she hadn't shown any sign of caring from the day he met her, Peter would have none of it. He was certain of the correctness of his beliefs, not even being willing to call them beliefs; to him they were clear and accurate perceptions. He dismissed my observations with a condescending air. Clearly he was affronted, and defensive about the notion that she might not be secretly yearning for him as he was for her. But saving face was important for him. He clung to his sense of the order of things, as to a dogma. Sadness never broke through to the surface as he maintained a bland, affectless, but earnest demeanour. Peter would acknowledge only that my comments were theoretical possibilities, but bore no relationship to his situation.

Peter and I had a different sense as to why he needed such a set of beliefs. He felt that the only way he could gain access to the lost Jeanine was by ferreting out the message and the meaning of all these stimuli. I felt his belief system was an attempt on his part to hide the hurt, sadness and loneliness he must be living with. Again there was no visible response.

I persisted, commenting on his condescending attitude towards me, questioning the certainty of his perceptions, telling him I knew that it seemed clear to him, but perhaps that was just so that he wouldn't have to deal with painful feelings like loss and rejection. Could his relationship with his authoritarian father be part of the scenario? Could there be some link between the conviction that he was being kept by Harold Geneen from seeing his true love and his authoritarian father's influence in his life? To all of this, he responded politely and dismissively, as if I were too dumb to even merit a response.

And what of the possibility that he was using denial and projection as a protective defence? Could his sense that the autocratic, powerful father was keeping him from his lost love be a way of not dealing with Jeanine having given him the wrong number, whatever that meant? Again my questions were met with disdain.

What of the secret language which was constantly revealing to him that he was being kept from his desired love? Was this a way of trying to stay one step ahead of the hurt? Could the theme of being kept from the person he wanted to be with have much to do with childhood, when there was some closeness with his mother, and the sense that his father, the arbiter of work and diligence, was somehow keeping him from his mother and whatever warmth there had been in that relationship? He thought not.

So it went, for the better part of a year. I questioned; he dismissed. I listened; he elaborated more paranoid revelations about Harold Geneen keeping him from his daughter Jeanine. I tossed out alternative explanations; Peter sneered. I talked about projection and a lack of clarity on his part as to the difference between inference and implication; Peter stuck to his guns, insisting that it was I who didn't understand and was confused. To me, Peter seemed to be no clearer in his thinking, still unwilling to look at the possibility that he had descended into a disturbed way of thinking and acting. Why was he seeing me? His family had told him to, and he thought talking with me would help him figure out how to get to Jeanine.

I thought he was unimproved, certainly frustrating, and was prepared to settle in for the long haul, hoping to help him live a less constricted and limited life. It seemed to me that there was a therapeutic relationship: he did come in for appointments, and this probably served to salve some of his loneliness and solitude. But suddenly Peter announced that he had a job offer elsewhere, and asked me to write a psychiatrist's letter detailing what situation he might work in. I was incredulous and attempted to tell him that this was premature, since he hadn't worked for two years, but here too he would have none of it. He had hit upon physically moving away from the pain as a means of dealing with the emotional hurt of his life. We discussed these themes, but his mind was made up. I suggested that if he did move, he get into further therapy, for the issues he had come in to discuss were unresolved. Thinking that he was far too disturbed to work, I penned a letter saying that he was subject to confusion in his thinking, and should only be hired if he could be adequately supervised in a supportive situation. To my surprise, he was hired and moved on.

One year later I received a letter from him telling me how much he enjoyed the job and thanking me. A little later there was a communication about being promoted. Seven years after seeing me, he sent a very nice note telling me how meaningful the therapy had been to him, and how helpful it had been in straightening things out for him. Exactly what these communications mean is unclear to me. I still have no idea how straightened out things are for him, no sense as to whether the pursuit of Jeanine continues, or if it has faded into the background along with other paranoid ideas. As always, Peter's sense of things is paramount: if he feels better, then that's the way it is.

The important lesson for me was that a psychotherapy which appeared to be stalemated and going very slowly (or nowhere at all) helped a delusional man reorganise to the extent that he was able to go on and function. Perhaps the relationship we forged together was most important; perhaps the exploration and delineation of his beliefs against the reality I portrayed was essential. Perhaps there was an empathic connection to me underneath his rejecting and extremely controlled facade which helped him overcome his isolation. Perhaps psychotherapy was his way of making contact with another person, and in the process examining the underlying hurt and projective and paranoid mechanisms he employed to keep from such pain. It's even possible that underneath his aloof and disdainful demeanour, Peter took in the interpretations and comments I made, some of which might even have been on the mark. But like all good card players, he played with a poker face.

CHAPTER TWELVE

Maya, Little, and the world of illusion

W orld view is the result of the developing child's behaviour and fantasy interacting with the environment. Repeatedly harsh responses at an early age in a particularly intelligent, creative and sensitive individual can lead to an underground and hidden delusional split in her sense of herself. Such a fragmented psyche undermines her very personhood, her sense of volition and her ability to observe herself and others. Once she is delusional, it becomes impossible to cope as a unitary being in the world. A fragmented psyche destroys her functional ability and makes it extremely difficult for consistency in thought and behaviour to develop.

This was the case with Gretchen, a woman now in middle age, who was an adolescent when I first saw her early in my psychiatric training. She had come in for some vague difficulties in life: trouble with school work, resentment towards her divorced parents, occasional suicidality, lack of motivation, depression and self-mutilation. These issues required twice weekly psychotherapy and were gradually ameliorated over the course of a year.

She was a tough-talking, intense and provocative, hippy-style girl. She was obviously intelligent and creative, wrote dramatic and sensitive poetry, and had a good sized chip on her shoulder. So far, she was indistinguishable from most of the rest of us. There seemed to be more, however. She would sit for hours without moving, unaware of where her attention was. She had unpredictable periods of depression. At times, for no discernible reason, she would cut herself. She had no idea as to why, no idea of what thoughts or fantasies were going through her mind at the time, nor any idea of what led up to this masochistic behaviour.

I raised a number of issues. Where did the depression and cutting herself originate? When did these episodes occur and in what circumstances? Could she be bipolar? She was not always depressed, certainly not when there was the stimulation of another person. Depression and self-mutilation occurred only when she was by herself.

Gretchen was the middle child of three. Her early childhood was punctuated by fights between her parents, and their divorce when she was six. She recalls her mother's physical and verbal cruelty during the time she lived with her mother alone, from the age of six to eight, and her relief after the age of eight when she lived with her indifferent, often absent father and beloved, old country grandmother. Her grandmother was the stable, loving figure in her life: highly religious, fervidly believing in life after death, and prone to praying devoutly throughout the day.

She couldn't stand either her abusive, narcissistically preoccupied mother or her callous, self-involved and removed father. Her main source of love was the grandmother who baked and prayed and turned to God repeatedly in trying to raise her increasingly rebellious granddaughter. Unfortunately, her grandmother's turning to God seemed so bizarre to this precocious and questioning girl that she ended up feeling even more isolated and unable to talk within her family about whatever was bothering her, whether school or boys or feelings.

Gretchen had not come in to treatment voluntarily. The family knew an eminent therapist who had, early on, realised the difficulties within the family and had served as a Dutch uncle to all of them. As Gretchen deteriorated during the late sixties, a time when the world of all families was subject to intense bombardment and attack, this kindly therapist insisted to her and her family that Gretchen get some treatment.

She stayed in treatment for the better part of a year. Her symptoms diminished, she appeared to be less depressed, and seemed to have the cutting under more control. As I attempted to get her to talk about what was going on in her mind during the times she was silent and withdrawn, or after the times she had previously harmed herself, she became increasingly combative. Any comments about resistance to doing therapeutic work were met with a flip comment about how she didn't have any other problems, she didn't need any of this authoritarian bullshit, no one was going to tell her what to do, she was better and she was out of here. And so she was out of therapy, without doing what I recommended, which was talking for a number of sessions about her wanting to stop treatment. She left without any chance to work through her reasons for leaving and taking a closer look at what issues were running her.

I was surprised that she was leaving. After all, I was about as counter-cultural as a psychiatrist could be in those days. There must have been underlying issues that prompted this "flight into health", but what they were I could only dimly guess. I was disheartened at the result of this therapy, certain that something more was going on, and somewhat irritated that my helpful attempts to make sense of what was going on had been discarded so abruptly. It was a useful experience in my training as a therapist, though, for with some resignation and thought and discussion of the case, I understood the power of the defences and satisfied myself with the knowledge that she was superficially better, her more severe symptoms having gone into remission during the course of treatment. I contented myself with the sense that perhaps she'd seek therapy again in some other setting.

Ten years later, Gretchen called. She had been married for nine years to a man who verbally and physically abused her. Just as her mother had tried to keep her in line when she was young with yelling and hitting, her husband did the same, venting his frustration and trying to control her. Unable to fight back or remove herself from the marriage, she had been mutilating herself over the years with razors, forks, knives and other sharp shards or implements. She was in such distress that she braved dealing with whatever she had fled from a decade earlier and began to take a closer look at herself. She feared her husband would find out she was in treatment, and so felt even more anxious about therapy than she had years before.

Initially, she had little sense of what was impelling her to harm herself. Again we looked at the masochistic-seeming, self-mutilating acts. Gradually she came to realise that she cut herself to express rage and fury at her current tormentor. When she was young and angry, she'd be silenced by either her mother's angry outbursts or her father's withdrawals. Now she had no outlet for the anger she felt at her husband and took it out by digging into or cutting at herself. As the blood flowed, like tears and powerful emotions that she could not express, she felt a slight diminution of her inchoate, unarticulated agony.

There was more to the picture, though. At times Gretchen was quite anxious, apprehensive about something she didn't understand. At other times she looked withdrawn and confused. Sometimes she was depressed and suicidal. This type of behaviour had been going on for much of the time since her previous therapy. Under the stress of the abusive relationship with her husband, she had slipped into her old patterns, with anxiety and confusion compounding the situation.

At times, during sessions, she was withdrawn and depressed in the office. Sometimes she acted like a young girl—meek, silly, impish, and playful; at other times she seemed like an age-appropriate 29-year-old woman. At times she couldn't remember what she had previously been doing. There began to appear a lack of continuity in her self-presentation and self-representation.

As we explored this area, it became clear that she felt to herself— and in the mirror looked like—the self she felt she was. When feeling like a kid, she looked like a kid; when feeling like a mature adult, she looked to herself, both from the inside and in a mirrored reflection, like an adult. She alternated in her view of herself, from grown up to child and back again. To be more precise, she did not see these fractures in her self-image as fragments of her being. She saw them as separate beings, each with a life of her own. For example, when feeling young, she was "Little", a three foot tall six- or seven-year-old, both in her mind's eye and in her mirror reflection. "Little" was controlled by the "Yelling Lady", who shouted at her and threatened to hit her if she didn't do as the "Yelling Lady" ordered. In fear of the "Yelling Lady's" criticisms and shouts, "Little" would try to placate her by cutting herself or making suicide attempts. At other times "Little" would withdraw further into her confusion, trying to regress to a womb-like state, attempting to escape an internal critical voice she felt was outside herself.

Gretchen tried to escape from what was clearly an internal voice by withdrawal and regression to what seemed like womb-like security.

She put all the bad mother frightening attitudes and criticism into the imagined being of the "Yelling Lady". This "Yelling Lady" was outside her "Little" self, or to be more precise, her sense of herself as "Little".

Why would anyone delegate away from their sense of self the ability to function and negotiate the world? Why did Gretchen dissociate? The answer is a combination of transference fear, powerlessness, and apprehension about what would happen if she got angry with her persecutor. Gretchen repeated past emotional and psychological reactions to painful events, perhaps in an attempt to master them, more likely in terror-filled repetition, like a compact disc or record stuck in a groove that has been gouged too deeply.

Just as she was unable to fight effectively with her mother or her abusive husband, as "Little", she was unable to resist the condemnations of the "Yelling Lady". In order to barter intrapsychically with the "Yelling Lady", Gretchen, believing she was "Little", had developed other "people" such as the "Efficient Lady", the "Competent Lady" and the "Sexy Lady" to help her deal with the "Yelling Lady" and function in the world. For example, when identifying herself as "Little", she would see herself as withdrawn and cringing before the abusiveness of the "Yelling Lady", all the while writing cheques or weeding the garden as the "Competent Lady". If she entertained, it was as the "Efficient Lady", while "Little" cowered internally.

In short, some of her attention stayed fixed in the childhood trauma of her relationship with her mother. She unwittingly repeated her traumatic childhood interaction with her mother internally, not realising that she was a person repeating, through intense delusional metaphor, experiences of her own childhood. And in the repetition of it, both internally and in her marriage, the situation worsened.

Again, hard as it is for us to conceive of it from the outside, this was Gretchen's perceived reality. To her, this dissociative delusional belief in "Little" and the others was as valid and natural as any of our beliefs, for it had always been this way, "as long as I can remember". This "reality" had been with her before her parents divorced, during the two years with her mother and the subsequent years with her father and grandmother. It had been there throughout school and her marriage. As her marriage deteriorated, she regressed more and more to "Little".

Parenthetically, and not too surprisingly, her "reality" had been there when she saw me previously in therapy, although it was never mentioned. As we got closer to what was going on in her mind ten years earlier, she was terrified due to both a desire to talk and to a fear of talking because "Yelling Lady" threatened harm should she tell anyone about her. This accounted for her previous precipitous bolt from therapy. Rather than go against the edicts of the "Yelling Lady", Gretchen adhered to a position of not seeing what she was doing intrapsychically, and left therapy rather that upset her internal, extremely fragile balance.

As a child, Gretchen feared her mother and yearned for contact with her unavailable father. She wanted to please both parents, to have them love her. Since both parents were essentially unavailable emotionally, Gretchen often withdrew into fantasies. Being light in hair and complexion, with blue eyes, at age four Gretchen invented "Maya", an imaginary playmate with dark hair and green eyes—her total opposite—who would cheerfully answer her mother's questions and deal with the world for Gretchen. While Gretchen appeared to be responding to her mother and other people, it was just a portion of Gretchen responding, for she was withdrawn into her own feelings of terror, insecurity and sadness.

As far as Gretchen was concerned, there were two of her. One was "Maya", whom she believed other people saw and liked; the other was Gretchen, whom her mother screamed and yelled at. Hating herself as she felt her mother hated her, Gretchen began, some time before her parents divorced, to believe that "Maya" existed in reality, as in her invention. When asked a question, "Maya" responded while Gretchen remained "Little" in her own mind. "Little" was different from "Maya" in looks and personality, and remained hidden behind "Maya's" responses. When she lived with her mother, the "Yelling Lady" became a fixture in her mind, as she dissociated and regressed even more firmly to the position of "Little" in response to her mother's attacks. By the time she lived with her grandmother, the "Yelling Lady", the embodiment of the harsh critical maternal super-ego—the punitive voice of the mother—was fixed in her mind.

Having returned to therapy now, we began to explore her beliefs. Gretchen became increasingly conscious of her articulated split view of herself. Even though it seems so clear to us, she believed she was many people, not one person with different imaginative attitudes. I viewed her as a unitary being who had tried to escape external reality and intrapsychic pain by unwittingly fragmenting herself as a way of distancing herself from the terror she felt around her abusive mother. As she became more aware of the disparity between her view of herself as many separate people and my view of her as one person who had dissociated at an early age to avoid fear, pain and sadness, she became more upset. This was not startling, since she had maintained a status quo, albeit an extremely disturbed and self-destructive one, for a number of years. The threatening of the status quo was unsettling, for she began to feel more of the upset she normally tried to avoid via the device of dissociation to different personae.

As the tension between her decades-long view and the view I presented to her heightened, she became more overtly suicidal. The "Yelling Lady", if anything, became stronger and threatened to kill her. Gretchen, as "Little", wanted to escape; if death was the only way, then so be it. The "Competent Lady" and the "Efficient Lady" were no match for the raging "Yelling Lady". They abdicated, leaving "Little" to face the music. Clearly this was a very dangerous situation. I increased our meetings to as often as necessary, in an attempt to quell the harsh internal voice; antipsychotic medications were available to her, as was the hospital, but were not necessary.

During this tenuous time, I actively interpreted the origins of the internal figures, reality tested about her internal figures being fantasies as opposed to actual beings, and emphasised the dissociation that had taken place more than twenty years earlier to escape an untenable situation with her mother. It became clear that Gretchen had regressed to a sweet little girl self, "Little", who couldn't express anger and wanted someone to take care of her. To be angry would mean punishment and abandonment by both her mother and the "Yelling Lady".

Gretchen's own anger increased, first at me for saying all these ridiculous, meaningless things, then at her mother for terrorising her for so many years. She hadn't been able to use that voice of anger, stolen first by her mother, then by the "Yelling Lady", then by her husband. Soon she got angry at me for not leaving her alone, for not leaving well enough alone, then she was angry at me for my mixed up impressions.

From her viewpoint, a strange thing began to happen as she screamed at me. Her suicidality diminished, the "Yelling Lady" became less intrusive and controlling, and "Little" became more in charge of her own life. As Gretchen accepted her anger as her own, actually as "Little's", the "Yelling Lady" left.

For a short time Gretchen thought she was still "Little", now free of the "Yelling Lady". She became more and more angry at me, as I kept pointing out that "Little" and all the other imagined beings were merely a way of maintaining a childlike sense of dependency and irresponsibility. "Little" and the others were Gretchen's attempt to keep herself away from angry, hurt and at times erotic feelings. From my perspective, she was Gretchen, not "Little".

For many years, Gretchen had identified herself with "Little", no matter what the mirror reflected to her, or what the situation. Having had "Maya" do the work for her in childhood, she remained "Little". Externally, "Maya", the "Competent Lady", the "Efficient Lady" and sometimes the "Sexy Lady" dealt with reality for Gretchen, as she believed that she was really "Little" cringing before the "Yelling Lady".

She would have none of my comments and interventions to the effect that she was the mirror reflection of Gretchen, not a young girl named "Little". She vehemently said that I was the disturbed one and I just hadn't got it right. I persisted, though, with comments about her childhood attempts to intrapsychically flee her mother's abuse having led to the origin of her split sense of herself as "Little" and "Maya".

Imagine her surprise when, after two weeks of this type of inter-action, "Little" vanished along with all the others. She felt exceedingly strange and vulnerable without a carapace of delusional reality to protect her from life and her own feelings. As we worked on her new found state of presence in the moment, suicidality and self-mutilating behaviour ceased. As she accepted her feelings as her own, Gretchen's confusion cleared, as did her behaviour.

Alone, Gretchen saw herself for the first time in twenty-five years as a person in the world. She no longer felt the need to flee feelings through the self-deception of fragmenting herself and splitting into a number of beings. She held her feelings as her own, not those of other and imaginary people. Gone was the harsh, punitive superego concretised and reified as "Yelling Lady". She no longer felt herself in thrall to the ever present and omnipotent "Yelling Lady". She no longer cringed internally. When she looked in the mirror, she could see that she was her full height, no longer the three foot tall child. Gretchen became able to act in the world as we worked on the therapeutic issues of her retreat from her own feelings and giving power to others, real and imaginary. She soon divorced her extremely abusive husband. Later on, she remarried and has since raised four children and maintained a family life and compelling interests.

From time to time, Gretchen would come in to talk of life and the tendency to regress to a state of being "Little". This urge would come up when she was having a difficult time and wanted someone to take care of her, even if that someone was an invented, imaginary being. Being alerted to her propensity to create imaginative, protective beings, she realised it was far easier to discuss these issues psychologically than to immerse herself again in her past beliefs. Through these intermittent psychological tune-ups, Gretchen realistically got the caring she craved in a more acceptable and realistic way.

Gretchen keeps in touch from time to time; she appears to be doing quite well. She operates on the independent side of the dependent/independent axis. Having lived so long as "Little", it is important for her to try and manage on her own. Needless to say, it would be no surprise if she returned to psychotherapy at some point in order to deal with ongoing life issues, or with a regressive pull toward previous modes of thinking. Hopefully, any upsurge of this type will be handled as it has in the past, through an intensive dynamic psychotherapy aimed at making clear the origins of any dissociative delusional retreats.

There are all levels of delusional disorder; paranoid delusional disorder is among the worst. Gretchen's disorder was a more easily treated one. In fact, as dissociative disorder, it is viewed as a neurotic, not psychotic disorder. Yet Gretchen suffered from a delusional disorder in the sense that she believed in a false internal reality existing in the external world. Her firm conviction of the real existence of her internal constructs of "Little", "Maya", "Yelling Lady" and all the others led to a debilitating disorder in which she couldn't tell real from not real and couldn't separate internal reality from external reality for more than twenty years. But whether Gretchen is viewed as neurotic or psychotic, the same intensive dynamic psychotherapy would be appropriate: clarifying, taking a history, and weaning her through an intensive exploratory dynamic psychotherapy from the fixed delusional beliefs that had threatened to wreck her life.

CHAPTER THIRTEEN

Death, Egyptian style

The following is a short vignette of a young man who had been delusional from the age of ten. It was a short therapy, perhaps a year and a half, punctuated with hospitalisations of several days' duration when the patient was seriously suicidal, but it does provide a look at the emotions and psychological anguish that can lead to delusion formation.

Some people live to be dead. Such was the case with Daniel, a thin, pinched, blond, sad looking young man in his early twenties who was preoccupied by the desire to die. He had a traumatic upbringing in a small town, had been molested at a young age, and was felt to be "queer" by the local townspeople. He had made several suicide attempts in his adolescence, had a number of psychiatric hospitalisations, and was given shock treatment at the age of sixteen to try to rid him of his homosexual urges. Needless to say, by the time he moved to San Francisco he was in terrible shape. Even though he was accepted by the gay community, Daniel could never accept himself. He was preoccupied with death, wanting to kill himself. And try suicide he did, numerous times, numerous ways. Towards the end of my psychiatric training, we met in a crisis clinic after one of his many overdoses.

We came to that interview from opposite poles and vantage points. He was dressed in purple, with a long sash dangling from his waist and a necklace portraying (he told me) Nekhbet, the winged Vulture Goddess, the Lady of Heaven; a scarab ring was on one finger. He spoke most deferentially, always calling me Sir. But I quickly found that his mind was keen and active.

I asked what he was preoccupied with, for he seemed to be looking off into space. Daniel was delighted that I asked, told me no one had inquired before, and proceeded there and over a number of sessions in my office to tell me in his clipped drawl of his cosmology. He was an Egyptian, not a present-day one but an ancient one. His name was Merit, formerly a princess in the reign of King Amenemhet III. He had returned from the land of the dead to inhabit this "poor boy" I saw in front of me. He had come to help the boy in need, in early grammar school. He had come back from the land of the dead where he had rested for thirty seven hundred years to help this "poor tormented soul".

I listened and asked exploratory questions, trying to get Daniel to flesh out what he was talking about. For it was Daniel talking, but talking as "Merit", in a deep sibilant voice, as one would expect a princess from the underworld to talk, especially if she were long dead. It all made perfect sense to me, confusing as it appears. It was comprehensible to me because it seemed likely that this was a way that Daniel, with my questioning and listening, could explain who he was and what he thought and how he had developed such ideas. This was even more likely, since Daniel had never talked about his certainty of the existence of "Merit" within him; now he was telling me his deepest beliefs.

In the afterlife, "Merit" was a spirit, feasting on the offerings that had been given her centuries before. Life was blissful, with many other souls who were friends and confidants. Before her death "Merit" had been a princess, much loved and courted, but she had died in her early twenties of some disease. Even though "Merit" had been a woman, she referred to herself as he throughout our acquaintance.

"Why do you refer to yourself as he?" I asked, quick to follow the lines "Merit" fed me. "I'm he because I am a spirit, neither he nor she; I'm he because I inhabit this poor boy," he replied. If that was good enough for Daniel and "Merit", it was good enough for me. I listened. Daniel, as "Merit", then proceeded to regale me with particulars about the court of the pharaoh and the nature of his life and death thousands of years before.

One day, while enjoying himself in the Egyptian equivalent of Valhalla, a spirit came to "Merit", telling him that this "poor boy sitting in front of us", a lad from another time, was praying to Isis and Horus. He, the spirit of "Merit", returned from the afterlife, for this was a unique event, a youth praying to gods long considered dead. There he found Daniel all rolled up into a ball, lying on his bed, sobbing with his eyes closed, praying to and invoking the gods "Merit" had known for many centuries.

"Merit" took pity on Daniel and infused himself, as all shades can, into the living boy—about ten years old, he responded to my question—and the rest was history. For the last eleven years, "Merit" had helped Daniel further his study of "Merit's" gods and goddesses. No matter what Daniel's parents did to him, no matter how cruel the other schoolchildren or townspeople were to him, no matter what drugs or somatic therapies—including insulin shock and aversive conditioning—were given to Daniel by ostensibly well-meaning mental health professionals, "Merit" was there to ease his distress.

It was a sad tale, with much embellishment, told in a voice that might best be called rural sepulchral. As the tale unfolded, there were many suicide attempts and a few short hospitalisations, for Daniel was trying, with "Merit's" help, to get to "Merit's" promised land, a place of peace and blissfulness where Daniel would no longer have to feel himself the "queer" and "faggot" he had been labelled in childhood.

Drama was Daniel's middle name. Repeated phone calls, over-doses and threats to harm himself were usual for him. Sessions were chaotic, with frequent races to the door to prevent Daniel dashing out to harm himself, and several episodes of taking sharp imple-ments away from him. The goal was to keep him contained enough so that he could talk about and work through the underlying delu-sions that were both so understandable and so destructive. When Daniel wasn't trying to kill himself, he retreated to the afterlife. He would spend many hours a day in a foetal position, certain that he was with the Egyptian pantheon. There he was accepted in a way he hadn't felt accepted whilst growing up, and couldn't feel accepted and acceptable in the gay community.

As I began to interpret to him the benefit of his belief in "Merit", I knew I was embarking on a dangerous task. If Daniel too quickly gave up "Merit", who consoled him, there was the strong possibility that one of his suicide attempts might prove to be more serious. If he didn't recognise that "Merit" was the concretisation of an imaginary construct created unwittingly to help the ten-year-old boy out of a very painful situation, he might stay preoccupied with death and the afterlife and repeatedly try to harm himself.

Within several weeks of talking about the defensive and consolingly protective nature of his belief in "Merit", Daniel began to let "Merit" go. He began to recognise what he had done to comfort himself, cried a great deal, and began raging at the various people who had been so cruel to him. Gradually, over a number of months, he came to see himself as a phenomenally creative young man with sexual identity issues who had never been accepted. He became an integral part of the gay community, and very productive.

During the course of his treatment he began to do serious work in his chosen field. Towards the end of his treatment, he crocheted a beautiful wall hanging on the motif of his Egyptian cosmology. It still hangs in my office, a reminder of his working his way out of a pernicious delusional system that seemed to have him fixated on the world of death.

Several years ago, nearly twenty five years after I last saw him, I received a letter from him. It was the nicest letter, detailing the work we did together. For me it was a pleasure to realise the treatment had helped and that he was still alive after all this time. From the letter it sounds as if my "deeply resonant voice, guiding him" may have replaced "Merit's" sibilant tones; perhaps he consults his version of my voice when unsure of the direction in which he wants to go. If so, it's not a bad way out of delusions, even if it's somewhat incomplete.

Here too, an intensive, psychodynamically oriented psychotherapy freed a young man who was apparently "untreatable". Years of delusions, constant suicidality and repeated hospitalisations faded and ceased as Daniel talked about his beliefs in the container of psychotherapy. The lasting benefits of taking a history from the delusional figure couldn't be clearer.

CHAPTER FOURTEEN

Nobody

Occasionally a chronically suffering, deeply disturbed person, with diagnoses ranging from paranoid schizophrenia to schizoaffective depression to bipolar disorder, will respond to a more exploratory, uncovering psychotherapy, even if it is of short duration. Such was the case with Pamela, whom I saw in consultation for fewer than ten sessions. She was a professional woman in her mid-fifties, well educated, and married. She had made a number of serious suicide attempts, had hospitalisations both long and short, and had recently been in the hospital for several months after a suicide attempt. She had seen another psychiatrist for four years, as well as other therapists, with no amelioration of a worsening condition of auditory hallucinations and delusions which had persisted intermittently since college, when she was found shouting at the voices that pursued her. Most recently she had slashed herself in a serious suicide attempt leading to a hospitalisation where high doses of several antipsychotics and antidepressants were instituted.

Pamela's psychiatrist was away for two weeks and asked me to cover for him and see her. He explained to me that she had grown up in a family of alcoholic parents. Over the previous eight months, she

had begun to talk to him about five or so episodes of sexual molestation by her father occurring at the age of ten or eleven. These upset
her terribly as she recalled them. In addition, she had begun to talk
about "Nobody", a Sasquatch-sized and shaped furry beast lurking
in the room, calling her a whore and a slut. He felt, as did the psychiatrists at the eminent centre at which she had just been hospitalised
for two months, that she needed increasing amounts of antipsychotics to contain her terror and apprehension.

In fact, in our first session, Pamela looked terrified. I asked why
and she started to talk about "Nobody"; he was in the office. She
acted like a cowering child being berated by this huge monster.
This was the key: the transference powerlessness in the face of the
blandishments of the harsh punitive figure excoriating her. I asked
why she adopted such a frightened posture. Since she could relate
the berating beast to her father criticising her, didn't she have other
feelings about "Nobody" or her father? Why was she only frightened? Where was her anger at him? She didn't know.

Before she left the first session, she asked for some homework. I
explained that I was a little concerned about giving her homework
since she had made such a serious suicide attempt, but if she felt she
could handle it, I would suggest writing about her anger at her father
for the molestation. She then asked if I would see her at a reduced
fee; I inquired as to who was paying. She and her husband were,
and the insurance; her father, having admitted his guilt about the
molestations, was paying the rest. I responded that I was angry at
her father just hearing her story and had no desire to cut my fee for
him. She seemed delighted. "Why are you so happy that I won't cut
my fee?" "It'll mean my father will have to pay the difference."

The next session Pamela was elated. She had written about her
anger at her father for the molestations. When she was in her pre-teen
years, he would sunbathe in his boxer shorts as she did in her bathing
suit. She describes him seeming to be asleep and suddenly masturbating and pressing himself all over her. She was terribly upset and
protested, but he said it made him feel good and he loved her. Four
or five more times, the same thing happened.

At this point, she told me that "Nobody" was in the corner of
my office. I asked her if she had any idea why "Nobody" was there;
Pamela had no idea. I asked if she could talk to "Nobody", but she felt
too frightened. She definitely wouldn't go over and say something to

him. I got up and explained that "Nobody" was just a figment of her imagination, but since she was so terrified of "Nobody", I would take her part and show to her that such a beast didn't exist except in her imagining.

"Is he here?"

"No."

"Here?"

"Yes."

I wave my hand about and she screams "He's all around you!" I explain that it's like a hologram at Disneyland. She has created the hologram and for good measure has added an auditory component.

"Is the beast talking?"

"Yes."

"What's he saying?"

Again he calls her a slut and whore. I step back and tell her that I'm play-acting in her holographic projection of her own fears and concretised symbols; I do not see any monster or believe in its existence other than in her mind. I reiterate that she is playing the passive and powerless transference child to the powerful monster representing those who abused her. For emphasis, I call the father to task for his treatment of her so many years before. Abruptly, "Nobody" disappears.

I ask about "Nobody's" origin. When "Nobody" had appeared six months previously, she had been very frightened, both of the intensity of his being and of his critical swearing comments. In addition, she was terrorised by "Nobody" cutting off the head of "Little Pamela". In response to "Nobody" she felt frightened, passive and powerless. From another perspective, when feeling passive, powerless and terrorised, she would project "Nobody" externally and feel the way she did as a molested child, rather than try to understand why she felt the way she did.

Could "Nobody" cutting off the head of "Little Pamela" have some meaning to her, I asked, but she could not answer. She was so immersed in the hallucination and delusion of "Nobody" that she trembled and remained in a panic. In the face of her creation "Nobody", symbolising her father, she had retreated to a frightened and dissociated state, unable to use her mind to understand her vivid metaphor. I continued with comments about her dissociation from the pain of the molestation and her concretisation of that act in the delusion of "Nobody" ripping off "Little Pamela's" head.

Pamela then told me how her older brother had molested her at about the same age. One night he had sneaked into her bedroom while she was sleeping and stuck something into her vagina. She had awakened with a start and started screaming. Her brother ran out and she began to cry. Her older sister heard her crying and came in to comfort her. When Pamela could, she told her older sister what had just happened. At this point the older sister had pulled the brother out of bed and started to scream at him, telling him never to do anything like that again. He didn't. Unwittingly, I had acted like the protective older sister when I had play-acted fighting with "Nobody".

Who was "Nobody"? "Nobody" had qualities like the father's criticism and the older brother's swearing. Most likely he was an amalgam of both of them. When "Nobody" suddenly disappeared, Pamela became frightened of him reappearing. I assured her that since "Nobody" was her creation she might create such an imagining again; but at least she had begun to establish a beachhead from which she could call her creations and projections for what they are, her own concretisation and exteriorisation of psychological issues and symbols. She caught a glimpse of what I was saying and relaxed.

Pamela's task then became to integrate her new-found insights and gradually reconstitute. Rather than cower in fear, she began to learn to use her intelligence to limit and eradicate her projected and terrifying psychic tormentors. What had been an insoluble psychological difficulty began to change as an ounce of courage replaced pounds of fear. An understanding of the origins of her delusional projections was the catalyst that led to her beginning to look at a complicated and life-threatening situation that had previously been too chaotic for her to actively integrate. She started to incorporate my abridged insights about projection and terror in the face of her projected and concretised fears. The terrors of delusion were transfixed by active psychological understanding. I hoped that in the usual "two steps forward, one step back" style, the delusions would fade and cease over a period of time.

In her next session Pamela started by saying that "Nobody" wouldn't be here today. He had come up that morning and she had banished him on her own. This was a milestone for her. Instead of cowering as she had for the last six months in the face of a concretised projection of whatever shifting, sliding representation "Nobody" might be at a particular time, she had felt the strength to own her projection as her own imaginative invention and had demonstrated the courage to rid herself of it. In the process, she had learned that her own psychic contents could be under her control.

A delusional presence like "Nobody" doesn't just appear. Most likely, there is a long history of disturbance in thinking and reality testing. Such was the case with Pamela, as I found out when I asked about imaginary companions. She had many imaginary companions as a child, ranging from "Mr Giraffe" to a panoply of friends. They never did fade out, and in fact became accentuated in her early teens. She would go off to a pond and play by herself, but in her reality, she was actually playing with her imaginary friends. Unsurprisingly, she retreated from thinking about the molestations by enacting many happy scenes over and over again in her fantasy-ridden, concretised reality. When the voices began talking to her at college, she was shocked that classmates and doctors made such a fuss about them; she didn't really understand that others couldn't hear them.

There was always a background of commentary from multiple voices; sometimes it was faint, sometimes intense. Somehow, in Pamela's numerous hospitalisations and previous psychotherapies, she had not received the clear message that these were her own creations, representing something from her own psychological life. Furthermore, she had the distinct impression that positive voices of warm, fuzzy delusional creatures were okay. My sense is that she had not asked if they were okay, trying to keep the good, close ones as she battled with the harsh, critical, negative ones.

I could not resist such an opportunity to state the obvious: these voices, just like "Nobody" or imaginary companions, were just that—imaginary, and of her own creation. I continued by observing that her family life was very stressful. Not only was there an alcoholic, sexually abusive father and a molesting older brother, there was also an austere grandfather who would stick a fork in a child's arm if he or she moved in an unseemly way at the dinner table. In addition, when another sister told the mother that she too had been molested by the father, the mother slapped her across the face and told her never to tell such lies about her father.

Here are some other examples pertaining to Pamela's psychological state from early on in her life. When she was four, her father put on a Halloween mask and jumped out of the bushes at her; she almost fainted with terror. The mask was then put under her bed until Halloween. Each night she would be certain that some man with a face like the mask would jump out at her. Many years later, she was certain that such a man, looking like a troll, would jump out from under a bridge on a pathway though the woods. When Pamela was eleven, her older brother exposed himself to her; she just "froze". When her older brother, at around the same time, tried to put something into her vagina as she pretended to be asleep in bed, her father excused his behaviour when another sibling told about it, saying it was no big deal. Again, Pamela lost her sense of what was right, froze and went on automatic pilot, retreating to a delusional and hallucinatory reality.

To counter such painful circumstances, I explained to her, she had broken with generally agreed reality, going off to the warm and compensatory pleasures of her imaginary companions. Unfortunately, whenever there is such a break with reality and the invention of positive, comforting delusions, there can be an upsurge of negative components of the psyche, as in the example of the many years of voices commenting, screaming and tormenting her. Suicidal ideation, suicide attempts, hospitalisations and fractured functioning and relationships were the result of the compact she had unwittingly made with herself. Once having broken the bonds of generally agreed reality and started believing in positive delusions, she was fair game for any of her psychic processes.

This is the essence of what must be done with a delusional patient: make clear that either good or bad delusions or hallucinations are destructive. The good delusions are destructive because they beguile and take the person's energy away from external life. The bad delusions—critical, negative, berating and intimidating— leave the patient cowering and unable to function in reality. Such a simple explanation must be spelled out over and over again to take root in the psyche and aid the transformation from a bedevilled, chaotic, psychotic state to a more sanguine, realistic approach to life. It helped with Pamela in half a dozen sessions, after a lifetime of delusions, hallucinations and altered functioning.

The way back, I told her, was through an understanding of the life circumstances that led to the dissociative and projective manoeuvres. In addition, she needed to become clear about the mechanism of withdrawal of energy from the painful external world and the projection of psychic energy into an unreal and imagined, seemingly protective and consoling world. She was a very smart woman; she understood the obvious, and for the remainder of the time with me continued to reintegrate. As she left one session, she added, "I've always felt that I was a nobody. Maybe 'Nobody' represented some part of me too." I told her I thought that was very likely and we should continue with that next time.

The questions I have with this woman who has made such great strides in just a few sessions after a lifetime of disability are the following. Could an attempt at a psychodynamic confrontation and exploration of her delusions years earlier have helped her, and had it been tried? Why wasn't it tried? Will the results persist? Her previous and current therapist did a great deal of reality testing with her, but apparently not enough genetic and historical reconstruction about the meaning of both voices and "Nobody". Neither he nor the hospital had emphasised the obvious fact that "Nobody" and the voices had internal and projected meaning to her which could be deciphered.

The wish to be rid of "Nobody" and the voices was conflicted, however. Half of her wanted to be rid of "Nobody" when he came at her with his penis erect, which he did some of the time. Half of her wanted to be close to him, when he would come to her with no genitals at all; at those times, though she could not touch him, she believed she put a heater next to him for warmth, or put a blanket on his shoulders. At these times she would feel warm and close to him. To Pamela these were real and intensely perceived. To her the world of "Nobody" had as much meaning as dinner with her husband. She had not tested the reality of this being. To her, "Nobody" existed and had terrorised her for six months.

I asked her to describe in some more detail the molestation by her father. He always sunned himself in boxer shorts; sometimes she would sun herself too, hoping that he wouldn't molest her. But he hadn't changed. He would take off his shorts, come close to her, and say she would make him so happy if he could just be close to her. She liked the closeness and making him happy. He was actually a very unhappy man, demeaned and criticised by his wife. At the same time as she wanted to run from him, Pamela sympathised with his plight, wanted to please him and comfort him; the sense of being special in his eyes was an added bonus. She was very frightened at pursuing it further. Had she thought during all those years of chaos that "Nobody" could be a symbolic representation of her father? "Kind of, but not really."

This is so crucial. For patients to change as Pamela started to change, reality testing is vital and the meaning to the patient of the delusions must be explored again and again. Pitfalls, detours, resistances, denials and evasions will be the patient's course; we must counter by repeatedly making clear that these are understandable phenomena, until the patient finally gets the picture. After years of confusion, Pamela got the picture in less than two weeks of reality testing coupled with an exploratory understanding of the meaning of her delusions.

Several weeks later, both Pamela and her treating psychiatrist told me that she was doing very well and that the gains of insight had lasted. "Nobody" had vanished and voices were handled as her own productions. With psychotherapy, the voices should diminish further as the underlying emotions are recognised and accepted as her own and the attendant psychological material is worked through. The chances are that the process of clarity and regression will be repeated a number of times until she finally fully accepts that she is responsible for the delusions and hallucinations which had terrorised her for so long. Finally, however, she has a key to unlocking and healing what had previously been an unfathomable, deteriorating and overwhelming situation.

With exploration, a condition which had required repeated hospitalisation and high doses of antipsychotic and antidepressant medication was beginning to change. Had I continued seeing her, I would have attempted gradually to lower various of Pamela's medicines, in an effort to see if she could continue to use her developing awareness of the projection of her own traumatic history and psychological issues onto alleged voices or "Nobody" to guide her through the maze of her own psyche. Little by little, I would hope that she would develop increasing ego strength and less and less terror of, and belief in, her previously life-threatening delusions.

My concern though, is that the gains of psychotherapy for these two weeks will not really last. As a therapist, one must be convinced that the work of defusing delusions can be successful, and try to clarify through reality testing, psychodynamic understanding and exploration with the patient what the whole disturbance is about.

Unfortunately, at the risk of being considered a "true believer", most therapists are not as convinced as I am of the healing benefit of such an approach and reconstruction. I doubt that such a severe disturbance can be turned around with such a short-term approach. Most likely Pamela will lose the gains of our visits. To achieve a more beneficial resolution might require a number of years of the approach I've delineated. In this situation, I could only wish her well and hope that enough interest had been elicited in the origin and unreality of her delusions to spur her and her therapist on to a more prolonged and potentially healing course.

CHAPTER FIFTEEN

The voice didn't win

Rachel was a petite, wan, twenty-year-old young woman with blond hair over her face when I first saw her on the psychiatry ward, after her third hospitalisation in eight months for serious suicide attempts, self-mutilation, and psychotic behaviour. As she had been after the other suicide attempts, she was withdrawn and hallucinating; she looked blank, her attention on inward preoccupations. On two previous occasions she had overdosed; this time she had been found, dazed and confused, wandering on the Golden Gate Bridge. There were reddish lines on her forearms from cutting at herself with a safety pin.

Rachel didn't particularly want to talk to me, but I had been called in to see her since she was on such a downhill, negative course. Her family was concerned that they might lose their daughter during one of these psychotic and suicidal episodes. Initially, Rachel was mute as I sat quietly with her. Gradually, she talked reluctantly, still immersed in whatever she was seeing and hearing. In response to questions, I learned that she was the eldest of four in a business family, with a sister 16 months younger and twin brothers five years younger. Her father was seen as authoritarian and rigid, her mother as inhibited and too tolerant of her father's tyrannical behaviour.

"You seem to be focused on something internally; if you are, can you tell me what it is?" To me, she appeared to be hallucinating, looking intently off into space in a preoccupied way. Rachel couldn't respond verbally, but was clearly very upset and moved to the corner of the room, where she cowered like a bullied child. She couldn't talk about her internal experience at this time. I put her on antipsychotics, and kept her in the hospital for several weeks as we tried to talk, and then tried to work with her as an outpatient while she lived in a halfway house. Of course, Rachel was hallucinating then and outside the hospital, even on high doses of antipsychotics; she just couldn't talk about it initially.

Thirty years later, Rachel described her first awareness of the voice in a way she couldn't begin to articulate at the time. "This realisation [that there was a voice telling me what to do] didn't come until several months after I started therapy with you. I was driving on the highway and I had to pull over because I was shouting out loud at myself, 'You should kill yourself!' over and over. That was the moment when I realised that something abnormal was going on. Until then I hadn't noticed how separate the voice acted and I hadn't recognised that there was anything unusual about having that kind of ongoing conversation, let alone a conversation that was so unilaterally vicious. So there was some shock in noticing what had been going on for a long time."

Before coming to San Francisco, Rachel had been attending a prestigious university in the Midwest, but she had dropped out because she couldn't handle her increasing anxiety and panic about meeting her own very high standards for academic performance. She believed her "job" in the family was to achieve perfection in school. Deciding to kill herself in a few days was the only way she could get a break from the anxiety: if she were dead, school would no longer matter.

Rachel had had several boyfriends in high school; she had limited sexual activity to making out because she had no intention of becoming pregnant. At the end of her second semester of college, she spent one night with a boy she liked, but didn't enjoy the sexual experience, which she stopped short of intercourse. This made her think that she might be a lesbian, and she decided to move to San Francisco to find out whether that was true. She had not been sexually involved with anyone, however, since arriving in San Francisco.

Rachel enrolled in a new school in San Francisco. It was, however, no better for her, as the panics continued. In the new school, she became more confused as the voice urged her to kill herself whenever she had assignments due. Any attempt at school work would terrify her, since she felt she had nowhere to go but down.

A few months later, a man sexually assaulted her at knifepoint and talked about wanting to kill her. Rachel was terrified, but pulled herself together enough to talk him into letting her go. She was physically safe, but felt defiled and hated men. The next day, filled with rage and self-hatred, she burned her arm.

We tried to understand the origin of her controlling voice. Rachel had kept a diary for years and, when she looked back through her diaries, it became clear that she began to speak to herself in the second person, as "you", in the eighth grade.

In high school, an internal harsh voice arose that told her she wouldn't pass tests, with the result that she procrastinated until the last minute. In college, this mode of dealing with pressure persisted and increased, with great panic around tests and papers and critical internal negative statements to the effect that "you'll never pass. You're a failure!" Again, Rachel talked to herself in the second person.

After the sexual episode at college, the voice began to criticise her for her sexuality, telling her that she was terrible for any type of sexual feelings. When she discovered masturbation in college, the voice became insistently more negative.

Rachel couldn't talk about why she cut herself. She was just upset. I asked how she felt, but she couldn't articulate either her feelings or whatever was going on psychologically. She couldn't even talk about guilt, her emotional state being so fragile and intense. I wondered aloud if there could be any relationship between her suicidal behaviour and self-mutilation on the one hand and her sexuality or feelings about her sexuality on the other. She thought not. She had no idea why she was terrified of sexual involvement, since there was no recollection of any sexual trauma. (Years after ending our work, in another psychotherapy, she came to the realisation that her father had sexually abused her when she was a child.) The voice gained increasing power and control over Rachel, sharply castigating her as "nothing," "fraudulent" and "disgusting." Hurting herself seemed to decrease the tension and agitation brought on by the critical, punitive voice.

Shortly after the assault, while sitting in a session with me, Rachel suddenly went blank; her gaze became fixed and she appeared to be responding to something internal. My attempts to get her to talk were of no avail. Abruptly, Rachel stood up and dramatically raced out the door, shouting at me that she was going to kill herself. Quick as I could—not so quick any longer—I followed after her in a Keystone Cops routine, chasing her for several blocks until she let me catch her. For her safety, we continued our outing; our destination this time was the hospital psychiatry ward.

In the hospital, Rachel told me that the voice had been getting stronger, urging her to kill herself. After ten days, on higher amounts of medicine and an exploration of her suicidal thoughts and actions and the delusion of the power that the voice had over her, Rachel stabilised. This time, though, she refused to go to the halfway house she had stayed in after her previous hospitalisation. The laws of California being what they are, and with Rachel saying she was no longer suicidal, there was no option but for her to return to the apartment she shared with roommates.

Within several weeks, she started a new job, where she functioned quite well. Most of our time was spent on the pressure and distress she felt at the job, and since she appeared to be worsening, antipsychotic medicines were increased to try to diminish her intense panic. I was worried about her and insisted she call me over the weekend to let me know how she was doing.

The next day, Saturday, Rachel called to check in from her apartment. She was cagy and evasive. I pushed to find out how she really was. It soon became clear that Rachel was trying to hide her intention of killing herself. I continued trying to talk with her, attempting to provide some safety and protection for her over the telephone, but to no avail. "The voice is in control. I hate you for trying to keep me from killing myself. Now there is nothing you can do to keep me from my death!" she fairly screamed at me. As I tried to calm her and keep her on the phone while my wife called the police on another line, Rachel became increasingly furious at me, her parents, and herself. In a bombastic, stentorian tone, she yelled, "The voice has won, the voice has won!" and raced out of the apartment, leaving the phone off the hook.

I shouted into the phone for a few minutes and finally roused her roommates. I urged them to search the apartment for clues. Just as the police arrived, the roommates found a series of suicide notes to me, her parents, and her friends. Piecing together the information in all the suicide notes, it became apparent that Rachel planned to jump off the Golden Gate Bridge the next afternoon at 4 pm. Although there was an all-points bulletin out for Rachel, I still felt the situation was chancy. Tricky and angry as the voice aspect of Rachel was, there was no guarantee she'd go to the Golden Gate Bridge at all; she might try suicide by another means. Yet she had said she was going there. I called the San Francisco police, the state police and the Golden Gate Bridge police to alert them to Rachel's plan, but didn't feel comfortable with that alone. It's so easy for someone to slip through the cracks in a life-or-death situation like this was becoming. I figured I needed some additional backup; now, where to find it?

Of course; the solution became clear to me. I called her parents, explained the situation to them, and recommended that they immediately go to the southern entrance of the bridge on the Bay side and wait for their daughter. If she showed up, they should corral her as quickly as possible and then yell for the police or Bridge Patrol to take her to the hospital. They quickly and apprehensively agreed. I had thought that both parents would go to the bridge together, but they thought differently. In those pre-mobile phone days, the father stayed home to monitor the situation and maybe get some phone calls about her.

By 8:30 that evening, Rachel's mother was on the bridge, standing guard. Sure enough, the following morning at 9 am, not 4 pm, Rachel walked onto the bridge, past the toll booths, unnoticed by any police presence. As I had suspected, Rachel didn't stick to the timing of her suicide plan. Having inadvertently given away her plan during the check-in call, Rachel abandoned the specifics of it. After spending the night outdoors, she started walking to the bridge in the morning—there was no reason to wait once it was light. Imagine Rachel's surprise when, after another hundred feet onto the Bridge, her mother grabbed her and marched her over to the police. Rachel was so dissociated that she made no response and couldn't even speak to her mother. Though mute at the time, Rachel eventually told me, she was certainly grateful to her mother later on.

During the subsequent hospitalisation, her fifth, a more detailed exploration was made of the compelling voice and her psychotic and suicidal regressions. It was a slow process. Initially, Rachel was near-catatonic for several days, trembling, often mute, despairing and non-communicative for the better part of the sessions. Suicidal intent remained strong; guilt about anything sexual continued to be intense. Rachel would run out of the hospital psychotherapy office and scratch herself, while the voice told her that she was horrible and disgusting for sexual thoughts. The voice threatened her with harm.

First, as we explored the voice, some attempt was made to help Rachel understand that the voice represented her guilt about sexuality. Her intrapsychic conflict was projected outside herself in the form of a harsh, berating voice instead of the internal superego attitudes most of us have. I reality tested that the voice represented her own thoughts and guilt, not the presence of an external, supernatural voice of an authority. The best we could come up with was that the voice sounded like her father due to Rachel's conflicts about right and wrong, put into the concretised form of her father's voice, criticising her and placed outside herself. During our work together, she gradually recognised that the voice came from her and represented her view of some of her father's values.

Secondly, the origin of guilt about sex was discussed. Rachel stated: "My mother doesn't want me to be sexual; my father doesn't either." Rachel had no idea why her mother wouldn't want her to be sexual. I wondered if she wanted us to talk with them about sexuality, but Rachel refused. She had no awareness then of any previous sexual trauma.

Thirdly, the origin of guilt about her anger at her parents, her father in particular, was discussed. Some family sessions were held in the hospital, in which Rachel raged at her father, then succumbed to overwhelming guilt, withdrawal, self-loathing and attempts to harm herself. She had no idea why she punished herself for her anger at her father. This theme of anger, then punishment for her anger, played out again and again.

Rachel had been medicated on reasonably high doses of antipsychotics. My experience, with the intensity of her voice and her dramatic suicidal urges and punitive cutting and burning, led me to the conclusion that the best that could be done was a gradual psychotherapy, slowly decreasing her antipsychotic medicines as Rachel gained control over the conflicted areas. In the best of all therapeutic worlds, Rachel would have stayed in the hospital for a long period of time. The best that could be done, however, was a six-week hospitalisation, with discharge to a halfway house.

Unsurprisingly, Rachel refused to stay in the halfway house after being there a week. She had again become suicidal, regressing to the voice, even on higher doses of antipsychotic medicines. The family couldn't fund the hospital forever; what could be done? Was this bright, creative young woman to go the route of repeated hospitalisations or custodial care in a locked facility? It just didn't make sense.

The solution to our dilemma was where it had been the previous time. I talked with the parents, explained the situation to them, and got them to agree to take her home. Both parents were highly motivated and concerned about their daughter. Although they were not terribly sophisticated psychologically, they were ready to work with me to provide an understanding, caring environment in which their daughter was not likely to harm herself seriously.

Rachel began dynamic psychotherapy with me three times weekly. Over the next five months, with occasional meetings and regular phone calls with the parents, she was able to titrate down and stop the antipsychotic medication. It was only used thereafter during a few life-threatening crises, perhaps ten times over the next year and a half of her treatment with me, as Rachel worked through and integrated her harsh superego conflicts which had been reified as the delusion of a berating voice outside herself.

The main thrust of therapy was to explore the primitive superego conflicts. Obviously, while she was living at home, there was a sense of Rachel's being cared for and nurtured, with many fantasies of being a little girl and of retreat to the womb. These fantasies were seen as yearnings to be free of conflict, close to her mother and, further, as a desire to escape guilt about sexual and angry feelings.

During these first five months, while she was on antipsychotic medication, Rachel had many episodes of withdrawal, tremendous outpourings of guilt and self-vilification as well as exacerbations of the voice, chastising her and urging her to suicide. Her guilt appeared to be about several things. She would rage at her father for the controlling things he did, then feel she was terrible for reacting and being so mad at him. In addition, she felt very uncomfortable about any sexual feelings and fantasies she had, berating herself for them. When either anger or sexual feeling came up, she would be likely to bang her head against the wall, cut or hit her left arm and hand and retreat into rocking in an attempt to comfort herself. Gradually, her self-mutilation of the left hand was understood psychodynamically as guilt about sexuality and masturbating. She retreated into hallucinations telling her she was bad when her guilt about anger and sexuality became too powerful.

There were a number of crises, several additional sessions, and times that the parents had to go on an all-night watch to ensure their daughter's safety. But the trend was towards Rachel understanding her thoughts and behaviour.

The general rule about psychotic patients is that when they come off antipsychotics they will regress and become psychotic again. Usually this is stated as a categorical imperative for maintaining people who have been psychotic on antipsychotics for life. Of course people are likely to become psychotic again; the trick is to interpretively explore the conflict-laden material, understanding full well that regression to a psychotic, delusional mode of functioning is likely to occur. What is necessary for the therapist is an orientation that delusions and hallucinations, like fantasies, dreams and imagery, can be interpretively explored and resolved.

Gradually, over a period of several months, Rachel timidly worked through rage at her father, finally yelling at him without decompensating after he made a remark that seemed inconsequential to everyone else. She carried on about his organising the world around himself and dealing with others in a guilt-inducing fashion in order to get his way. She carried on until she understood both the dynamics of her response and the extremity of her outburst.

Here too, there were a number of nights when Rachel would call frantically, saying that the voice was telling her to hurt herself, or after she had burned or cut herself. All of these phenomena were explored and dealt with interpretively and empathically and seen as her difficulty in dealing with guilt and anger, punishing herself rather than dealing with her anger at her father.

Over the next ten months of therapy, Rachel became more able to deal with her self-mutilation around the issue of anger; the voice became less present as an expression of guilt over anger. Extremely strong guilt and trepidation remained, however, around the issue of sexuality. There were frequent retreats into the voice and suicidal thoughts as we looked at the guilt Rachel felt about her sexuality. Often she would leave the office with the voice chastising her, after having volunteered some sexual thoughts or fantasies. Sometimes she would wander dazed; occasionally there were suicidal commands as an expression of guilt about her being interested in sexual things. At times, she needed a low dose of antipsychotic medication to calm down.

In phone calls after these periods, and in later sessions, the upsurge of hallucinations and suicidality was seen as a retreat from Rachel's own conflicts about sexuality and an attempt on her part to put the intrapsychic conflict outside herself in the form of the voice. Instead of a person with conflicting impulses and inhibitions, Rachel saw herself as being pursued by a deprecating voice coming from outside herself.

This type of material persisted for several more months, with Rachel taking two steps forward and one and a half steps back. She gradually became more intact, enough that she could travel with a friend for a month. She then returned to therapy for her last few months before returning to the school she had dropped out of three years before.

At this point, a very interesting episode occurred. Rachel came to a session ashen and tremulous. Slowly and tentatively, amid disclaimers, she told me what had happened. She had gone out dancing and couldn't take her eyes off the men's genitals. It upset her terribly that she could be interested in sexuality, especially men's sexuality. There followed several more retreats into hallucinations berating Rachel for her "disgusting" nature, followed by suicidal ideation. These were explored and understood as her desire to evade dealing with those aspects of herself that were interested in sexuality. Her all-or-nothing views protected her from the shades of grey and conflicting impulses that make up a more mature intrapsychic life.

There followed a number of terrified and disorganised episodes, which Rachel was able to see as her reluctance to accept an emerging interest in sexuality. As we talked, she began to tell me about the rules and strictures against sexuality in her family. As far as Rachel was concerned, her mother's attitude towards sexuality was only negative. I told Rachel that this was an intrapsychic problem; if her mother came in with her and reassured her that sex was all right, she would still feel guilty about her sexuality until she had worked through her own conflicts.

The very next session, Rachel brought her mother in with her, thinking I had suggested that her mother come in. After I pointed out Rachel's ambivalence about ameliorating her harsh internal attitude towards sex, essentially bringing in her mother on her own volition, the three of us discussed Rachel and sexuality. We had a very useful and clarifying talk. First, Rachel had accurately registered and then adopted some of her mother's tenets about sensual life. Secondly, the mother said that at the time she gave birth to Rachel's sister, she had quickly toilet-trained Rachel (then 16 months old) with some stern injunctions and comments about "that dirty area". Thirdly, Rachel's mother thought she was going to be pregnant with Rachel before her wedding day.

This information, although somewhat difficult for Rachel's mother to present, aided Rachel greatly in modifying her harshly critical attitudes towards sex. Rachel realised that her own mother's conscious values about sex were markedly different from what Rachel had fantasised these values to be.

Rachel became quite forthcoming in her discussion of her sexuality, bringing up dreams and fantasies and recollections about being interested in sexuality. She became able to masturbate without guilt, stopped retreating into hallucinations, and became quite interested in talking about many aspects of sex.

During this period of psychotherapy, Rachel was no longer psychotic. She had no delusions, no voice and no regressions to terrified self states and suicidal thoughts. Hallucinations, self-mutilating behaviour, regressive retreats and the upsurge of psychotic thinking had been understood as a retreat from intrapsychic conflict. They did not return during the remainder of treatment with me.

After several more months, Rachel returned to the university in the Midwest with the recommendation that she stay in psychodynamically oriented psychotherapy. Perhaps there were more layers of the onion to be peeled. Before leaving for school she presented me with a poem celebrating her sexuality, a first for her, since so much of her other writing over the previous years had celebrated death.

Three years later she graduated with honours and dedicated her thesis to me. That dedication told me that the gains of therapy were still holding then. The gains have continued over the intervening years. Significantly, Rachel remembers the most important lesson: we were able to deal with psychotic and suicidal behaviour through an in-depth psychodynamic understanding; such knowledge, wherever it leads, will stand her in good stead.

Thirty years later, when I tracked Rachel down to get her permission to publish this material, she told me several important things. Firstly, in a later psychotherapy with a woman, she uncovered memories of sexual trauma by her father. She said that it would have been too hard to discuss this kind of material with an older male psychiatrist, even if she had remembered it at the time of our work together. As several of the other cases in this book make clear, physical or sexual abuse can readily lead to the development of psychosis. I only wish that Rachel and I could have sorted out this material in our work together, but it sometimes takes a prolonged time to uncover and deal with such painful material.

Secondly, and most importantly for the purposes of this book, Rachel told me that since our work together she had had no hallucinations or voice telling her what to do. This young, allegedly schizophrenic woman took the insights of our therapy together and maintained her gains and sanity over the intervening thirty years, even uncovering painful details of trauma, without retreating into psychosis or needing antipsychotic medication.

Gracious and generous as usual, Rachel penned the following note: "You also have my deep appreciation for your efforts to change the assumption that people who need antipsychotic medication at one point will need to take that medication for the rest of their lives. I have benefited profoundly from your progressive perspectives about the role of medication in supporting therapy, not replacing it." Such a result is not only a testament to Rachel's intelligence and desire to understand herself but a further example of the transforming power and life-saving effectiveness of intensive psychotherapy in those once so disturbed.

CHAPTER SIXTEEN

The world-class artist of the symbolic world: the Mafia, the movie stars and the "Unconscious God"

A number of years ago a colleague told me that a man in his early forties, whom she had seen twenty-five years earlier while he was a student at a nearby boarding school, had contacted her. He had been at a famous hospital—let's call it Cotswald's—for ten years, continued to be severely paranoid, and wanted to leave. My colleague had discussed the case with the administrative psychiatrist at Cotswald's, read a number of treatment and discharge summaries, and decided that her half-time practice would not afford the best treatment for the patient. Uncomfortable with her former patient's therapeutic progress since she had last seen him, she asked me to take a look at the material.

The clinical resumes were daunting, with diagnoses like schizophrenia, paranoid, chronic on Axis I, and borderline personality as Axis II. To quote from the summaries after ten years in a hospital and halfway house setting at Cotswald's, "he demonstrated the same characteristics and symptom complex that were present when he first came to Cotswald's". In addition to his "ineffective coping outside a structured setting" the patient showed disordered thinking "dominated by a paranoid delusion that included receiving special messages from the television and radio and feeling that he could communicate (via an implanted transmitter) through his teeth and that anything spoken would happen [...] This made it extremely difficult to communicate with the patient at all." In addition to an "escalating daily franticness", the patient was frequently suicidal and had been so at the time of his last full-time hospitalisation at Cotswald's. This did not present an auspicious picture.

As I leafed through the material, I had a pervasive and discouraging sense that there probably were some people who couldn't respond to an intensive outpatient therapy, and this patient might be one of them. Luckily, a telegram from the patient to my colleague fell out of the envelope. It was filled with thirteen one-liners, each funnier and more provocative than the last. For example: "Yes, I have received the fascinating records of ... and (check where applicable): (1) I have my full quota of paranoid schizophrenics; (2) I would love to, but I'm afraid of them; (3) I'm afraid of them, but I know love conquers all; (4) It's the Sabbath and I don't do mail on the Sabbath; (5) I don't do mail or windows." Something didn't compute.

I tossed around a number of questions and issues. Can a chronic paranoid schizophrenic have a sense of humour? At least the patient had something to work with. Was the patient's paranoia related to psychiatric institutions as well as to other settings? Why did he sound so recidivist in the psychiatric write-ups and so amusing in his one-liners? Was full-time hospital care required? Primarily because of my curiosity about the patient who had written the one-liners, I contacted Cotswald's and told them that I would see him for a week if he were able to come to San Francisco under his own steam, and was not too suicidal.

After interviewing the patient for a week, I found him so disturbed and so engaging that I decided to attempt an outpatient intensive psychodynamic psychotherapy. Cotswald's told me that they had done all they could up to that point and recommended that he continue to stay there, but they would acquiesce to the patient's wish to be discharged. They agreed to be available if the patient couldn't manage under my care. From their perspective he was "untreatable and unable to function outside the hospital in the long term". They recommended that he stay in the hospital for the rest of his life. Over the last eighteen years, with the exception of two short several-day hospitalisations early in his treatment, the patient has managed as an outpatient, as he has worked on and through delusional material which had been with him for the previous thirty years.

George

George was a tall 42-year-old man, who was initially dressed as if living in a time warp, with ill-fitting, old-fashioned and often shabby clothes from a different socioeconomic class. He was clearly terrified, spoke apprehensively and guardedly, and demonstrated the paranoid thinking and ideas of reference that had been described in the hospital reports. He showed signs of tardive dyskinesia; his fingers were gnarled and bent in the way characteristic of too much antipsychotic medicine for far too long. He was on 150mg. of Loxitane per day and had been on high doses of this and many other antipsychotics.

As always, I took a history from George in the hope that this would lead to my being able to make sense of how he got into such a profoundly disturbed condition. However, it was impossible to go from A to B with George. What was required was going with the delusional flow, asking repeatedly how such and such an idea began, what was going on at that time, and how he became certain of his conclusions.

Gradually, over a long period of time, a picture of interlocking and self-confirming delusions became clear. To demonstrate to himself that one delusional belief was true (the television talking to him, for example), George would support it with another delusional belief, such as the newspaper told him so, as did the passing car on the street or the checker in the supermarket when he said hello. All of these proved to him that the first delusional belief was true. Though the information came out in fragments, this is the gist of George's story.

He believed that his teeth were transmitters and receivers, that the Mafia, in conjunction with his father, both heard his every thought and implanted thoughts in his mind. He was certain that numbers were the Mafia's mode of communicating their displeasure, each digit meaning a different thing at different times. Colours and the media had also been enlisted by the higher powers, his father and the Mafia, to criticise and judge his response to the messages sent to him. He was convinced that he had been "framed" and that "bad things will happen" to him. He often spoke in a hesitant whisper, certain that he was being observed.

He was the younger of two sons, with a brother four years older who intimidated him and poked fun at him, two younger sisters, a tough but doting father and a highly critical, narcissistic mother. The parents would often fight about the mother's treatment of George. When he was in high school, his father began to see other women and his mother became increasingly disturbed, necessitating a several-month hospitalisation for psychotic depression when George was fourteen.

George, who had always felt unloved and unaccepted by his peers, his mother and his older, competitive brother, was sent off to boarding school after his mother came into his bedroom one night and threatened him with a pair of scissors. The parents divorced shortly after he left high school and his father remarried. Mother and older brother had nothing to do with George. Even though his father continued to care and provide for George, he was preoccupied by his new wife and family. George began seeing psychiatrists at the age of seven, for he was shy, inhibited, withdrawn and depressed. He saw therapists throughout the intervening years. He did well at boarding school, and continued on to college, from which he graduated with a degree in sociology.

George began smoking marijuana in high school, and by the time he finished college, he was extremely dependent on amphetamines, which he abused in large quantities. As a child he had been given medication for sleep and anxiety by both his father and a child psychiatrist; for him, instant relief from distress was through a pill, not through comfort and talk with his parents. Both parents warned him against getting fat, placed him on diets, criticised him for having dessert, and pushed diet pills on him from an early age.

By his mid-twenties, the cycle of psychiatric hospitalisations had begun, when his family realised that he had been eating from garbage cans for more than a year: in George's mind, if people threw food away it was fit for him. His favourite garbage bin was behind a bakery. For more than a year, he would go there several times a day, crawl in the bin and eat pastry and creamy fillings and frosting to his heart's content. At times he had to fight off homeless people who competed for the same food, but since this was his only secure food supply—the Mafia monitoring system could not enter the walls and cover of the garbage bin once he had burrowed in—he wasn't about to let anyone else take it from him. Since food eaten in the dumpster couldn't be observed by the Mafia, his father wouldn't know how much he was eating.

George had begun to believe that the Mafia was pursuing him, when he became convinced that his dentist, who happened to be his father's dentist, had implanted a transmitter that was being monitored by the Mafia at his father's request. Now he was certain that he was constantly observed, controlled, and told what he could and couldn't do. George believed that he would be punished if he did certain things, and generally lived under a terror of "bad things happening to me". He didn't know what the "bad things" or punishments might be, so imagined the worst: death, torture, dismembering. All bad things seemed likely, if not a foregone conclusion. The Mafia knew everything and would report to his father instantaneously every thought he had, and certainly every action he took. Every day he would awaken convinced this would be his last. His terror increased exponentially, with every conceivable negative and compensatory positive delusion imaginable afflicting him. As a result of his heightened anxiety, he became more and more mired in a chronic paranoid and schizophrenic orientation.

He had a number of psychiatric hospitalisations in the his twenties and early thirties, for up to a year at a time, as well as attempts at drug withdrawal. In a drug rehabilitation unit he became increasingly frightened and psychotic as they took him off antipsychotic medication. His paranoia and imaginativeness reached such heights that he was convinced that people at the drug treatment centre, and even the landscape of the drug treatment facility, were in league with the devil. Hadn't he just seen "Rosemary's Baby"? Hadn't the Manson cult happened?

Unexamined by him and unfettered by any type of psychological, antipsychotic or mood stabilising treatment, his beliefs expanded in a most self-referential and all-inclusive fashion. If something could happen, it would happen to him. If something could be thought, it would happen to him. Daily, he would be certain that he would die a terrible death. The fact that he hadn't died didn't reassure him; it just confirmed for him that he would die on the very next day in an even more terrible fashion. As his self-referential, boundary-less, fragmented and all-inclusive thinking increased, George's condition deteriorated markedly.

He was transferred to Cotswald's, a world-famous psychiatric hospital, where he stayed for the next decade. When he left Cotswald's, Axis IV read as follows: "Severity of psychosocial stressors: 4 Severe. Repeated hospitalisation for a chronic mental illness, with a developing awareness of the extent of his handicap (predominant enduring circumstance)". As far as they were concerned, the patient was hopeless after ten years of hospital care. He was "untreatable" and could only be maintained in a hospital setting, or live close to a hospital. He could only be maintained at best; intrapsychic growth and healing were considered to be out of the question.

Examples of the formation of delusions

George's delusions emerged in fits and starts; I will present a reasonably coherent description of them and their meaning to him, but we must remember that they became clear as a fragment here and a shard there, during the course of therapy. Each delusion was associated with powerful feelings of warmth and cosiness if positive, or terror if negative, depending on whether he felt the delusions were for or against him.

While in a drug rehabilitation unit, George had work done on his teeth again, and this time became certain that the Mafia and his father were now in cahoots. They began sending him messages: the license plates of the staff at the drug rehabilitation unit all had CO in them; George reversed it to OC and became certain that OC represented "organised crime", the Mafia. Soon he began to notice "syndicated" and "syndicate" at the end of columns or the crossword puzzle in the newspaper, and became certain that this was a sign from the Mafia, the syndicate. Lot numbers on the bottom of objects such as paper cups and plastic forks became signs that he was being observed, and that messages about what to do to him were being sent out by the Mafia to their henchmen in the form of a number code.

George's terror increased as he became certain that he was the object of full-time surveillance, monitoring and control. His father became associated with the Mafia in his mind, in part because he was from a large city which had a significant Mafia influence, and had moved some of his businesses to another city which was well known for crime. Rather than realise his own loneliness and craving for contact with family or friends, George developed a paranoid delusion of family involvement featuring his father and "The Family" of the Italian Mafia.

People began to look like others from the past. Rather than thinking that he was lonely and seeing certain similarities between people, George became certain that the higher powers were sending people from the past to him. When he asked these look-alikes on several occasions who they were, he was certain that they were lying to him when they denied knowledge of anyone from his past. He could no longer trust anyone, and believed only his mistaken and terror-ridden perceptions and conclusions.

These themes built negatively on each other. The interplay between loneliness, impulsivity in thought and action, all-inclusive thinking, certainty in the correctness of his own perceptions and lack of trust in others left him in a rapidly spiralling downhill course. Faster and faster, he became enmeshed in a labyrinthine maze of his own making, ensnared by his delusional orientation.

Here are some examples of his tortuous thinking. Dr X had a patient who George was certain was a witch. Dr X had another patient whom he had purportedly tried to seduce; she had both reported Dr X to the authorities and then come down with multiple sclerosis. George was convinced that Dr X's witch patient had caused the multiple sclerosis in the other patient as punishment for reporting Dr X.

At a halfway house he had been in, there was a man who was a child molester and said he had been in the Manson family (family again); he had a third nipple and said he was a witch. George became convinced that his father was a witch or sorcerer, because he had a third nipple. Convinced that the child molester in the wheelchair was a witch, George hit him over the head with a coke bottle. He began frantically to mull over the following questions: Weren't all people with three nipples witches, sorcerers and potential murderers? Hadn't his father rubbed his chest when George was eight? Might his father be a child molester? Hadn't George's father's first wife died before he married his mother? Wasn't his father pathologically jealous? Could he have murdered his first wife? Couldn't his father, as a witch, hook up with organised crime and observe and influence his every move and thought?

When he saw *The Stepford Wives* and *Rosemary's Baby*, he became convinced that someone was trying to clone him and kill him. This belief that he would die originated after he wished his stepmother would die a terrible death. George was unaware that his fear of death was a psychological retaliation for his murderous feelings for his stepmother and (through a slip in therapy) towards his blaming, criticising, neglectful and punishing mother.

The Stepford Wives were cloned when they got too assertive. By his account, anger was not encouraged at Cotswald's. If he was angry, he would be asked who he was really angry at, with an attempt to focus back on the transference aspects of his anger rather than let him experience and work through the angry feelings in the present. By his account, he wasn't encouraged to deal with feelings in a fashion that would help him learn to tolerate them. On one occasion at Cotswald's, he was allegedly placed in room restriction for six months after becoming extremely angry. Whether these are accurate accounts or not, his difficulty in coping with anger fuelled his retreat into reparative psychotic thinking and paranoid fears of retaliation.

George feared that something bad would happen if he ate a pizza while in the hospital. This belief worsened when he realised, two years later, that four years earlier a man had died of cancer in the same room in which he ate the pizza. Was his eating pizza responsible for the death years earlier? Missing boundaries, a lack of logic and timelessness characterised his thinking. Causality as we know it didn't apply. He could eat a pizza one year, find out two years later that someone had died four years earlier in the room in which he had eaten a pizza, and then proceed to relate the death to his having eaten the pizza two years after the person had died. Time and causality meant nothing to him. If it is thought, it is!

In another example, he could watch an *I Love Lucy* rerun forty years after the television show was made and be certain that Lucy or Desi or the director of the show had him in mind all those years earlier when the show was filmed. Time and causality were turned topsy-turvy as George was convinced that Fred Mertz was sending him a message from beyond the grave or commenting on his thoughts as he had them.

Such self-referential thought, such grandiosity, such turning the rules of logic on their head are a cardinal sign of these people's deep affliction. Rather than see the world of illusion as a creation of a frightened, lonely, primitive and terrified self, George tried to make sense of a worsening situation by convincing himself that he was correct and that he could trust no one else's perceptions and comments, only his own. He relied on a very disturbed psychotic person, on his terrified self, for guidance. He trusted and stuck adamantly to his own totally misguided perceptions.

Course of treatment

On moving to San Francisco, George immediately complicated any potential living situation by buying and insisting on keeping a cat, which meant that halfway houses would not take him; there was no choice but for him to live alone and unsupervised.

From the first interview, I tried to assess George's ability to develop an observing ego. He was convinced that his beliefs were absolutely true and had no doubt that his father, the Mafia and other higher powers controlled and monitored his every thought and action. He was also certain that if he said anything, it would come true and he would be punished.

After several sessions I began to say things to the effect that I knew he believed what he told me to be true, but that I thought there might be some alternative explanations for his view that his teeth were wired and his mind controlled. (I even sent him to two different dentists to have him look at the X-rays of his teeth.) Even though George was convinced he perceived the world as it was, I continued, our task was to help him understand how he got to see things as he did. I told him that I didn't expect him automatically to give up his beliefs, since they must mean something to him. Wasn't it curious, I went on, that he was so lonely and cut off from family and friends, yet believed that "the Family" and his father followed his every move? Could the extent of his paranoid beliefs be a reflection of the extremes of his loneliness? Could the paranoia be his way of trying to maintain contact with his family or other people? He hadn't thought about that, but was quite convinced that I must be mistaken.

I searched for an inroad into George's delusional thinking, something that would give us leverage from which he could view his disturbance. Two rather obvious ways presented themselves during the first few sessions: the regression to a younger self image when he felt frightened and overwhelmed, and the certainty that "bad things will happen to me". During the first few sessions I asked how old he felt when he was certain that his teeth were wired and his father and the Mafia were sending him messages. He said he felt seven.

"What happened then?"

"My mother would yell at me and hit me with the hairbrush."

"Anything else?"

"My father warned me that I would get fat if I ate too much; bad things will happen to me."

Bad things here meant losing his father's love if he got fat. He then elaborated with a verbal picture of a frightened, timorous seven-year-old self, cowering in front of his mother. This may seem a little stagy, but I was able to point out a number of different self images which were correlated with different frightened-feeling states and constantly associated in his mind with the phrase "bad things will happen". There was the three-year-old boy fearful of his father, the seven-year-old terrified of his mother, the infant in a crib, needy and longing for contact, and the nine-year-old fearful that his friends would ostracise him for stealing a baseball mitt at school. Stagy or not, it helped George gradually develop some nascent observing ego, as I repeatedly pointed out the regression to a younger self state and the associated feeling states of anxiety, loneliness, dependency and longing as well as the chronic fear that "bad things will happen".

Once it became clear that George regressed to feelings and actions which were correlated with different frightened self states, a beachhead was established from which a little rational perspective might develop. In therapy I would repeatedly point out the regression away from a forty-something self to the frightened little boy self. He didn't calm immediately, but I persisted, convinced that the pervasive thought disorders could be understood and worked through via a painstaking understanding of the origin of each of his mistaken beliefs. With this orientation, it was possible for me to deal with any countertransference frustration as I pieced together the various threads that had led to such a pessimistic-seeming and severe condition. Here are some examples of the coalescing and overlapping themes and threads that led to such a destructive picture.

The fear that George was being framed originated when his father once said a picture of his brother had a nice frame. Since George's uncle, whose picture was in a frame, had died of cancer, he was certain that his father killed his own brother and might try to frame George, and eventually kill him. George began to see "framing" everywhere. During the time at Cotswald's, he had become extremely fearful of his father and unwilling to talk to him, certain that he was the evil mastermind behind all these messages and plots. Previously, his father had appeared to be a bulwark against frightening feelings and delusions. This paranoia about being framed and the certainty that his father was an evil force was dealt with over a number of months with comments that the paranoia was his way of maintaining a family connection in the face of his extreme isolation.

One of the main hallmarks of George's self presentation was his extreme fear, leading to regression and paranoid thinking. His overriding fear was of his father and his witch-like powers. Here are several examples.

George told his father that he had to go to the dentist. His father said he had had a bridge for thirty years. George immediately thought that his father had a radio receiver and transmitter in his bridge, and that once George had dental work done, his father would be very tuned in to him, hearing his every thought and fear and protecting him from the allegedly evil people at the drug rehabilitation unit. At this point George felt extremely close to his father.

Whenever George said the word "jealous" in front of his father, he was certain that his father retaliated and "framed" him. In his mind, this was the result of his belief that his father was extremely jealous, and angry at George for using the word "jealous". The history of his father's alleged jealousy was as follows. The father's first wife had died of a stroke when she was six months pregnant, after telling him that she wanted to have lots of babies. As the father told the story many years later, he said he had said to his wife, "What about me?" As far as George was concerned, his father was jealous of his unborn child and had magically killed his first wife and knocked off many other people through his magical powers.

For a number of months, George's fear become our central focus as we unearthed more and more illogical, but (to him) plausible reasons to be terrified of his father and the Mafia. Gradually the fear abated, and George became able to talk with his father in person and on the phone.

George's lack of what we usually term logic, his different kind of logic, became a focus. His fragile boundaries, his grandiosity, ideas of influence and reference and his nearly instantaneous relating to himself of all types of events were discussed over and over again. George's denial of causality and time were stressed as being paramount in the development of his thinking. Repeatedly I emphasised that his mode of thinking left him in an intolerable and frightened place. Trusting his own perceptions as he did left him in the throes of an implacable paranoia.

Why did he regress to such a fearful state? Childhood tales and recollections came to mind: stealing a baseball mitt at school at the age of nine and being ostracised; feeling left out by the other kids from the age of six on; feeling different, less than them and treated as if he were strange; leaving class from the age of seven on to see the child psychiatrist; being hit by his beautiful mother at the age of seven; playing with animals as a child because they "didn't hurt me".

Numerous housekeepers came to mind, including a nanny who apparently tried to drown him when he was three. George recalled being his usual self, acting like a normal three-year-old, being silly and talking back to the nanny (who had been with them for a year) while he was taking a bath. Suddenly, the nanny held him under water so long that he thought he would die. He remembered the angry look on the nanny's face as she let him up and then pushed George back under the water. He remembered his mother rushing in as she heard the commotion, and the nanny saying that George had slipped in the tub and she had rescued him. George remembered being afraid to tell his mother the truth, out of fear that the nanny would do it again. He remembered being afraid, after the near-drowning episode, to express himself in his usual boisterous way.

George recalled the tension at home, the mistreatment by his older brother, the fights between his parents, the neglect and humiliation he suffered from his mother, and his beloved father always criticising him about getting fat. During therapy I encouraged him to assert himself, and at times George screamed and carried on in great voice, filling the air with increasingly violent metaphor. Although it is difficult to believe he was not encouraged to work through his

angry feelings in previous treatment settings, this was his conten-
tion, and a sad one if so, since projected anger clearly forms a major
aspect of any paranoid system. Our goal was for George to integrate his anger as his own, not as projected anger coming back at
him.

Attempts were made to make sense of George's life. Fear of death,
a sense of being controlled, isolation and loneliness were all preva-
lent themes. I pointed out to George some of the analogies, the transference themes. From the nanny who tried to drown him we could
extrapolate to the Mafia trying to kill him. From the psychiatrists he
saw from such an early age, the many years of hospitalization, and
the constant efforts of both parents to keep him from getting fat we
could extrapolate to the Mafia monitoring his every thought and
action. From the isolation, humiliation and estrangement he felt as
a child we could extrapolate to his feeling the very same way now.
George felt so controlled and threatened at home and at school that
it seemed to me that he had continued the early family constellation
and dynamics into his forties. He remained the controlled, constantly
monitored and threatened little boy, unable to assert himself.

From all these we got isolation, friendlessness and loneliness,
which he tried to turn around to the positive compensating delusion
of television and movie stars in loving relationship to him, as confirmed by whatever they are saying in movies or on television. If a
famous movie star said something to her leading man, George was
convinced that she was talking to him, through the lines of a movie
made years before. What a wonderfully heady experience! But then
other lines in the movie were directed against him: in George's mind,
people were jealous of his perceived intense relationship with the
movie actress he was convinced talked to him and responded to his
every thought and wish.

To deal with how badly he felt, George was reinterpreting everything as directed at himself. We call it grandiosity and ideas of
reference, but for him it was simply a continuation of his family situation, coloured and influenced by nearly fifteen years of being in the
psychiatric hospital and what he viewed as authoritarian treatment
settings. This interpretation in all its guises was made over and over
again: it was not reality that George was afraid of, but the extrapola-
tion of his familial reality of being controlled and terrified that he
projected onto the world. Rather than the external world, it was his

perceiving apparatus that was at fault. And it was at fault primarily because he transferred his emotional and psychological experiences of the past onto the current situations in his life. This was only one level of approach in dealing with his near-constant misinterpretation of internal and external life. In dealing with such a chaotic and disturbed person, with so many levels of dysfunction, one needs to be on the alert for the next area of misperception; and there were ever so many.

George's certainty that the media, controlled by the all-pervasive Mafia, sent constant messages to him via television shows, radio, advertising, newspapers and magazines was a major problem. I made up even more elaborate and equally consistent paranoid delusions to explain various numbers and perceived messages in the newspaper, radio or television, all the while telling him that these were my creations, just as his were his creations fuelled by the need for contact with others. I got him to laugh at some of my concoctions and, tentatively, at his previously firmly held beliefs. For good measure, I also questioned his conviction that numbers had meaning other than quantity. To George, thirty-three might mean she loves me, thirty-five might mean she dislikes me and forty-seven might mean a calamity is about to happen.

George was buried in a world of symbolic meaning, focused on himself in a grandiose, self-referential way. He could not conceive of the concept of symbolism, one thing standing for another. As far as George was concerned, one thing meant another in reality. And in his reality, the Mafia controlled and monitored and threatened. To compensate for this terrified existence, he had developed comforting delusions which alternated with his fears of the Mafia. Famous movie actresses and television performers were in love with him. They would speak to him as their movies or shows proceeded. Every phrase or gesture was interpreted as related to George and to his thoughts.

Living in this world of instant communication—boundary-less, unscientific, impossible and all too real—left George convinced that the performers he was in love with were always communicating with him. He could stay up all night, waiting for a particular movie star to show up at his apartment, for hadn't she said that she would in the latest movie George had watched? He could bathe, clean his place and dress in a most fashionable way, all the while expecting a famous actress to knock on the door and come in. When she didn't show, he didn't feel rejected. There was a war out there between the good, loving people and the Mafia. He became convinced that other forces, for example the National Organisation for Women, conspired against his meeting a woman, for they were jealous of him. Again, there was no awareness of the symbolism of the jealous mother or stepmother, nor of the projection outward onto others of his own internal difficulties. For more than fifteen years, since his drug experiences and nearly fifteen years of institutional treatment, George's beliefs had expanded to include every aspect of life as a potential persecutory or succouring message to him from the outside.

Little by little the conviction that the Mafia and his father monitored his teeth began to crack. Each time, the psychotherapeutic exploration of feelings, regression to a younger self state and projected impulses led to the resolution of these decompensations, without resorting to increases in medication or hospitalisation, although they were available if necessary. Sometimes the process of reintegration was accomplished in one session, sometimes over a few days or weeks. At times, the belief in the Mafia and his father controlling him reappeared, and would then diminish as we explored the relevant psychological issues and regressions. One particularly persistent delusion remained, however, a belief which had been instrumental in his staying stuck in paranoid thinking over the previous years of extensive treatment.

In his late twenties, believing himself to be pursued and controlled by the Mafia, George felt understandably terrified and lonely. His family or therapy situations offered no comfort, since they were all tainted with his paranoid beliefs. Only one person appeared to love him and really care for his welfare, a television talk show host. He was as certain that the talk show host sent him caring messages through the television as he was that the Mafia sent him frightening and evil ones. A confirming piece of evidence that the performer cared for him was as follows. He had once written for a ticket to his television show and was convinced that the performer had sent him two airline tickets to meet him in Ontario, Canada, but had sent the tickets to his father. What made him so certain of this? He had once seen two airline tickets in his father's hand, from Ontario airport in Southern California. To George's way of thinking, Ontario was Ontario, whether it was in the same country or not. In his mind, driven by the desire to see his caring talk show host, Ontario could have been Portland; he would have found a way to make it the same. Generally agreed rules of logic did not apply.

George lived in a world of his own associations. He was convinced that his views and associations were better than anyone else's. It mattered not a whit that he had sacrificed himself for two decades and had been in institutions for so many years. As far as he was concerned, he was correct in his perceptions, no matter how many well-meaning therapists and hospital staff members might try to get him to see things differently. What caused such a conviction in the rightness of his own perceptions? Could there be some meaning to his grandiose view that he was correct in spite of so many other people's view of things? What made him so certain that he was correct, in the face of all the suffering he had endured?

I raised these issues over a period of time, not really expecting any answer, but trying to drive a slight wedge into his firm convictions. I didn't expect any immediate results, but figured I had to try and get him to see both that he was paranoid and how such a belief system developed; perhaps through this course some of his frantic certainty that his associations were more right than other people's logic might recede.

George became increasingly upset and regressed, seemingly more and more firmly fixed in his paranoia. Knowing that one break with reality, even for a positive belief, can have far-reaching and destructive effects on all of one's thinking, I persisted in pointing out the regression to paranoid beliefs. I suggested that we contact the television performer, but he would have none of it. Eventually he agreed that the referring psychiatrist and he could write a letter to the talk show host. When a reply came back saying that the late night talk show host had never heard of him or communicated with him in any way, George's paranoid defences, already cracked and tottering, crumbled.

Needless to say, George was very sad and lonely without his delusion of instant contact with his favoured talk show host. For a while he insisted that the talk show host must have been blackmailed by the powers that be; otherwise he would have admitted his close relationship with George. To deal with his pain, George slipped into alcohol abuse, and used whatever drugs he could find.

Here the thrust of treatment was twofold. One was reality-oriented: stop the alcohol. The other was an attempt to understand the dynamic of why he was attempting to evade feelings again, this time with alcohol, as he had previously with delusions. One short substance abuse hospitalisation was necessary, as was repeated focus on his use of alcohol or stimulating cold pills to alter his mental state and mood.

There was also a long period of time, after he gave up the delusion of the talk show host, when George developed a fixation on a movie star. He saw all her movies on video, memorised all the lines, and inserted himself into her leading men's roles. Having continued a break with reality in the firm conviction that this movie actress was talking to him, it was a simple matter to believe that newscasters, television and radio shows and old reruns were sending him messages. He was in a constant state of excitement, fear and ecstasy. The figure-ground had broken down; he had no boundaries when it came to the media. Newspapers touted his every action and thought. Headlines blared his thoughts and monitored his every wish. Music was about his life and being.

Here are several examples from his years of treatment; they indicate how seriously disturbed he was. On one occasion, he was missing for three days, having had an episode of transient global amnesia (perhaps related to self-prescribed mind-altering substances) and spent three days sitting on a rubbish pile next to a large department store. On another occasion, while out for a walk with a nature group, he threw himself into the ocean and tried to swim out to a passing freighter, certain that a movie actress whom he had seen in a recent video was on a boat several miles offshore, awaiting him. Still later that day he got lost in the woods and was found by rangers, bedraggled and confused. He was in a frenzied world of his own creation. His break with reality was indeed as severe as described in previous hospital records. The question was how to defuse the power of his delusions and establish some observational point from which he could view what he was doing to himself. If a beachhead could be established, perhaps the whole house of delusional cards would begin to crumble and tumble down.

Several thoughts came to mind. How did the break with reality occur? If I could get him to talk about his sense of the first break with reality, perhaps some nascent observing self could begin to develop.

The first delusional episode he could remember happened when he was certain that the dentist had implanted monitoring devices. We had made some headway on the Mafia delusions, but he still spun out delusional thought after delusional thought, self-referential to the nth degree. His mind was a kaleidoscope of grandiose and self-referential thoughts and images. My sense was that there was more to the equation, perhaps some overriding break with reality.

Luckily, two things happened. Firstly, George developed a delusion that the referring psychiatrist was going to leave her husband and marry him; and secondly, he told me about the time he flew up to God. This episode of believing that he was going to get married to the referring psychiatrist (who saw him from time to time when I was unavailable) was instrumental in his realising how delusional he could be. Even though others could easily see that he was delusional, he had not previously fully acknowledged it, for to him he was uncompromisingly sticking with the truth.

George had felt more and more tied to the referring psychiatrist during the first several years of treatment. Once he thought he was driving to her house late at night and wandered into someone else's house. He slept in the playroom of this house for several hours, surrounded by the toys of unknown children, certain that his beloved referring psychiatrist would come downstairs to greet him. He awakened before dawn, realised that he was in someone else's house, and beat a hasty retreat, undiscovered.

George became more and more excited, enthused and possessed by the certainty that his beloved referring psychiatrist loved him in turn. He was certain that the wedding would take place on a particular Sunday afternoon, with photographers, caterers and a host of guests, none of whom he knew; but he would be married to the woman he loved, of that he had no doubt. (I knew nothing of this wedding delusion.) George spent the weekend in preparations, made all the necessary personal ablutions, dressed as nicely as he could, certain he was about to be married in full view of everyone in a nearby church. He arrived an hour early for the ceremony. In happy anticipation, he waited. When two o'clock had come and gone, his heart sank. He waited, hoping the bride had been delayed; perhaps these people walking by were the guests, also waiting. Hours passed. No bride, no photographers, no caterers. He was devastated, devastated enough to tell me the next day.

Painful as it was for George, this was an extremely valuable episode, for he could see how delusional he had been with a real person in his life. We called the referring psychiatrist, who kindly said that she was happily married and had never indicated in any way that she was going to marry George. She had had no intention of marrying him the previous day, or ever. With this information from a real person he could almost trust, George began to look at his penchant for delusion formation.

He had been so involved with the referring psychiatrist in his mind that he had consulted a newspaper as an oracle. If George had a question on his mind (Did a movie star love him? What should he have for dinner? Should he watch a certain television show?), he would consult the newspaper, open to any page at random, read a few words, and go from there to whatever thoughts and associations came to mind. As far as he was concerned, George was following and exploring truth, for he was dealing with his "God within" and the powers that be, who directed the newspaper to say whatever it said. In short, any thought or feeling or fantasy George had came from the superior "God" he kept within himself. He was always right and others were always wrong, for his God had told him so. This belief had shielded him from the truth of what mere mortals—friends, family, hospital staff and psychiatrists—had told him over the decades of his disturbance. George believed that whatever he thought was so, with the consequence that he was grandiosely secure at times and grandiosely terrified at others, depending on which way his associations went. If not his father's most loved child, he was his God's favorite.

This was the lucky second thread which, once explored, began to help unravel the knot of George's delusional thought: the belief in his "Unconscious God". This belief in his infallibility as the diviner of the meaning of the "Unconscious God" was one of the basic problems. It accounted for George tuning in to the idiosyncratic meaning of numbers, the oracular leaps of his mind in response to books and newspapers and whatever flighty associations he might have, all of which he regarded as his truth. In his mind, no matter what anyone told him, George was correct in his perceptions because only he could fathom the "Unconscious God".

Here was the way in to his delusion-making propensity. I seized on it, much as he didn't want to talk to me about it, and over a long period of inquiry and discussion, pieced together the following tale, which George believed was reality. More than thirty years ago, he was in a hotel room, loaded on marijuana and ingesting very large quantities of amphetamines. He was unhappy and feeling isolated; a previous girlfriend had committed suicide, and he was overwhelmed by the transition from college to the working world. He took more and more speed. Suddenly, George was not lying alone in an isolated room; he was in the starry firmament communing with God, being held by Him. God, the father, had chosen him; George was his chosen one. Finally, God the Father loved only George.

Haltingly, little by little, the picture became clearer. He was the child of God; he was Jesus suffering for our sins. Instead of being criticised by his own father, George was the favoured son of God. George very reluctantly gave me more and more titbits of his belief that he had fused with God and was his child. It became clear that his boundaries had collapsed; he could not tell "me" from "not me". He was subject to every stimulus passing in the breeze, and associated to them all as he tried to see the wishes of his father, God, and follow his will. This further accounted for his primitive and oracular reading of newspapers and magazines, for he was only divining the will of God in leafing through the pages and finding an oracular and prophetic meaning.

As we talked more and more about his belief that he was following the will of God in all his self-referential associations, his paranoid delusions began to melt. For some months we discussed the correctness of his reading of the "Unconscious God", and began to draw a link between his religious experience (on drugs) and his belief in the "Unconscious God". As long as George was following his "Unconscious God", he was certain that he was following the truth in the face of a world of falsehood. No matter what the travail, years of hospitalisation, eating from garbage bins, living in deteriorated circumstances, jumping in the ocean to see a movie star, overdosing (for he had done that too on several occasions), he was sticking with his God and the most intense experience he had ever known. In following and living out his associations as "reality", George was doing whatever he could to hold on to the experience of love he felt when held by "God the Father". If not his father's most loved child, he was his God's favourite.

The most intense and meaningful experience in his life had been his drug-laden religious experience. George's associations had the certainty of "divine revelation". The "Unconscious God" was equated with his unconscious. As far as George was concerned, thoughts, impulses, associations and feelings were all a manifestation of the god-head pulling him in every conceivable direction.

The problem was that George was immersed in the concept of "God within". He had no perspective from which to understand that these were his own yearnings and associations. To him, any associations or thoughts about whatever difficulty he perceived or anticipated were "God's writ". He lived in a world of "revelation". Here too, he retained a unique relationship to his "God". He was the most special, a priest of the divinity. Only George could fathom God's meaning as revealed in his associations to whatever situation might occur or whatever phenomena might ensue. He was Sybil to Apollo, the High Priest to Yahweh, revealing his wisdom. The only difficulty was that his was a one-person religion, scoffed at and disbelieved by others. What was wisdom and truth and essential reality to George was seen by the rest of us as gibberish.

Haltingly, George was able to talk about how one-down he felt in his family, how his other siblings were favoured by both of his parents. Slowly, he began to see that the "Unconscious God" devoted to George was a compensation for his perceived position of being less favoured in his family. As all these concepts were elucidated and discussed, we made the slightest inroad into fixed paranoid psychosis, that proverbial beachhead of rationality began to be laid down. Little by little, we explored his belief in the "Unconscious God" and all of its ramifications, including his delusional thinking and delusion formation. More and more clearly George began to see that he had been following his own promptings and wishes for a close relationship in his own family, and that he had not been following the dictates of an "Unconscious God".

With the delusional thought explored more fully, George began to reintegrate, even talking about and giving up the idiosyncratic meanings he gave to numbers. He began to recognise that fourteen was fourteen, not a message to a woman that he loved her. Ninety-three became that, just a number, and not a concatenation of different feelings all caught up with the two digits and their relationship to each other. As I kept discussing with him the mistaken premises that underlay his paranoid beliefs (e.g. the idea that people could know his thoughts, read his mind, and monitor his actions), a number of things began to occur. He became slightly more reality-oriented, but was still very paranoid. We explored every conceivable notion he had, reality testing and trying to understand the psychological significance and underpinning of each belief.

On one occasion, in great terror, he blurted out that the Walkman radio he often listened to was talking to him when he came into my office; we went round and round about what made him think the radio was talking to him, what stimuli had set off such a thought, since it was impossible from where I sat. How did he get to that thought? Why did he trust his beliefs and perceptions—beliefs that had landed him in the hospital for more than a decade and destroyed his life for more than twenty-five years? Why did he stick to his beliefs and assume the worst about the treating professions which he thought were in cahoots with the Mafia?

Over and over again we discussed these issues from all sides. Little by little a beachhead was established against his grandiosity and omnipotence. Slowly, ever so slowly, he began to talk about the hurt he had suffered at the hands of his family and, being so sensitive and unable to separate others from his own paranoid projections, the insults and pain of everyday life.

George elaborated on his conviction that he was God. He had believed it for more than twenty-five years, since his spiritual experience on drugs. Such a belief, as I had surmised, gave his life meaning, but also further locked him into paranoid distortions which only worsened an already fragile and fragmented existence. Who better than the "Child of God" to be "God"? Like a high priestess of an ancient deity, George had not only heard, seen and apprehended the "Word of God"; he had been taken over by his most beloved and become "God". Compensatory religious experience, an attempt to take him out of a most painful life situation, had been transformed into a firmly held paranoid belief system of twenty-five years' duration.

Reading the minds and intentions of others, George was certain that they could—if powerful enough—do the same to him. He oscillated between fearful and abject despair and persecution on the one hand and grandiose certainty on the other that he knew the will of God and in fact was immersed in him, was indeed the Deity himself. Having been frightened and isolated to begin with, he further removed himself from the workaday world and began a deteriorating course of twenty-five years of paranoid delusions, multiple long-term hospitalisations, confusion and intrapsychic chaos as he defiantly and defensively clung to the belief that he was God. No matter how great his suffering, it was acceptable to George, for he was suffering for man's sins as he led an increasingly tortured existence.

It was a trade-off. On the positive side, he was God, or God's child. He could communicate through the television and movies with anyone his heart desired, feel loved and included in the words of movie stars and television personalities. He could predict the future through the way he "read" magazines or newspapers, floating off to any association he made, certain that this was the "truth" of the "Unconscious God". On the negative side, George was terrified, subject to any torturing force he could imagine, believing that his teeth were wired and his thoughts monitored by the all-powerful Mafia with whom his father was allegedly in cahoots. His beliefs wrecked his life, forcing him to substitute imaginary relationships for actual ones.

Gradually, over a long period of time, he began to cry about his lonely, isolated position. His positive delusions no longer comforted him, providing solace against a life of pain and misinterpretation. As he wept, a more real person seemed to emerge. He screamed to me, "I'm no longer God"; "I'm not the second coming". "My defences are down now". There it was; George had laid it out for me. Somehow, most likely when he believed he had been borne up to God and held in his arms, he had developed the belief that he was God. Such a belief had inured him to the pain of life and further sequestered him from the pain of his grandiose and paranoid distortions of reality. I asked for amplification, but, sobbing, he told me he'd talk about it some other time.

As we discussed his plight and the defensive nature of his grandiose conviction that he was God, George began to weep and sob, and did so for a number of sessions. I stayed in close touch with him, to guard against suicide. This was genuine sadness, for he was not only giving up delusions which he had cherished for so long, he was also grieving about the waste of possibilities. Most importantly, George wept with the knowledge that he was not God and that he had been deluded. As he wept, he cleared, not all at once but little by little. There would be some clarity, then he would slip back. The process continued for a number of months as he took stock of his illness and his life, retreating to a delusional safe haven less and less frequently. The gains of psychotherapy began to take hold.

But he would sometimes slip back into delusions. We'd go over the material time and again. He'd seem out of it, but would then slide back into delusional beliefs. I began to call this delusional life "George-land" to help him distinguish it from generally agreed reality. He would deny that he had a private world he would go off to in order to avoid painful life circumstances, but one day an opening occurred. As with all delusions, I took a history of it and its development.

As we were sitting in a session, George waved. I enquired as to what he was waving at. We had been talking about a movie actor who he was certain hated him. Reality checks and discussion did little to move him from the belief that the actor, who was going out with an actress whom George loved, hated him. Oedipal interpretations about mother, stepmother and father, extrapolated and projected anger, although probably correct, didn't turn him away from the conviction that he was in communication with this actor and actress. However, the wave and our discussion of it turned the tide towards reality. After many evasions and segues, George slowly told me that he had been waving goodbye to the actress we had been discussing. Slowly, he agreed that he lived in an altered internal reality, "George-land", much of the time, and had done so for nearly forty years. It was at times a safe place, filled with those things he didn't have in life: loving friends and movie actors and actresses, even God.

As we searched back, George was able to say that he had had such a place in grammar school, where he had felt so isolated and alone at the age of eight or nine. It had developed when George felt the other children thought he was strange. He believed at the time that if he stole the baseball mitt of his schoolmate and played baseball with it, he would become the friend of the boy he had stolen from and bask in the warmth of his and his family's friendship. This was more than just wish fulfilment. George was certain that closeness and friend-ship and warmth would be the result of his stealing the baseball mitt, unlike the coldness and sarcasm and humiliation he felt in his own family. To his shock, he was further ostracised and talked about by all the other kids when it became clear that he was the thief of the baseball mitt. Needless to say, this drove him more deeply into "Georgeland", a world of imagined compensatory relationships. At high school and college he had some friends, and lived much more in the world of reality, his inner world becoming less important to him. But once out of college and thrown back on his own resources (the situation complicated by increasing drug abuse), George began to spend more and more time in his inner reality, "Georgeland".

Until we began exploring "Georgeland", it seemed real to him. He could be sitting by himself or talking to someone at the hospital where he had been for a decade, but in his mind he was with a previous psychiatrist or a famous actress or television personality with whom he was certain he had a longstanding relationship. His consciousness was split, and in this split state, George's internal reality with relationships, warmth and love took precedence over any external involvements. To him, the internal "Georgeland" had much more depth, emotion and warmth than any surface involvements with other people. He knew it to be true, yet had enough sense to keep his inner world hidden from others.

Rather than cathect the external world and relationships with actual people in his life, George immersed himself in his internal delusional world. While watching television more than twenty years earlier, he had become convinced that there was communication back and forth with the television characters during the following episode. A maternal political leader running for office asked the question on television: "Do you want help?" George responded out loud, "I want help." This was followed up by the politician saying, "I'll help you any way I can." With this, George became certain that there was one to one communication with television characters, who soon began to populate "Georgeland", and with whom he had his most intimate relationships. It was a short step to seeing meaning in numbers, reading books in a self-referential way, and seeing newspapers and ads as comments on his thoughts and behaviour.

It was only through our thorough exploration of the origin and meaning to him of "Georgeland" and the judicious use of psychotropic medication that George began to grow and change psychologically, but an obstacle still stood in the way. Little by little, it became clear that he did not regard the problem as one in which he was sometimes in reality and sometimes in delusion. As far as he was concerned, the distinction was between good and bad realities, between pleasant, exciting preoccupations on the one hand and painful concerns on the other. For example, it was a good thing in his mind to be preoccupied with, and talk to, a movie star on television.

It was a bad or painful experience to stay in a lonely reality. For him a good reality was to be in a positive delusion; a bad reality was to be in a painful delusion or an unhappy life situation.

As we teased apart this mistaken categorising of his life's experiences into good (positive delusions) and bad (negative delusions or painful external reality), George became clearer about his constant delusion formation. He wanted to live in a pleasant reality at all costs, even at the cost of his sanity and in spite of many years of treatment. Slowly, protesting all the while, he changed his categories to delusional and non-delusional.

Then a terrible period of fear enveloped him. For as long as I knew him George had been afraid that he would die on a particular day; such a belief had persisted for more than twenty-five years. As he cleared, George confided in me that he was certain that he would be killed by the Mafia for having told his secrets. Once aired, this delusion too faded away as he became more confident that not only the belief in the Mafia monitoring him, but the certainty that the Mafia would kill him for talking about them, were just creations of his own imagining.

Finally George felt solid enough to begin to confront life. He began to see how he formed delusions at the slightest provocation, and started to live with fewer of them. After twenty-five years as a paranoid schizophrenic, the psychotherapeutic onion had been peeled to such an extent that his psychological energy turned away from the hollow internal preoccupations he had believed to be reality and towards the external world. For the most part he appears to have given up his delusions, although he holds on to loving feelings towards a certain actress who was once the focus of extensive delusions—but instead of being psychotic about her, he is a fervent fan. His vitality and verve have re-emerged. George is now fully able to acknowledge that his previous beliefs were paranoid. I wouldn't be surprised if he should slip again, but that is to be expected in this type of long-term therapeutic process.

George re-established contact with his father and stepmother; they were on good terms for years before his father's death. George also dealt with his mother's death without the necessity for re-hospitalisation. Delusions have resurfaced at times of stress to offer him comfort, but have repeatedly been seen as his imaginative way of trying to bring meaning and love into his life. The danger of maintaining positive delusions, of course, is that positive delusions may go hand in hand with negative, terrifying ones.

During the last number of years, George has gained a great deal of perspective on and often given up his paranoid beliefs. He lives independently, has made friends, and reads as others read. This previously "untreatable" man, who was told by Cotswald's that he couldn't live outside a hospital setting, hasn't been in a psychiatric hospital or day care for more than fifteen years. His idiosyncratic, homeless look has been replaced by an interest in fashion and the latest styles.

At times, George slips into delusional thinking, but for shorter and shorter periods. Each time, we go over the questions of whether or not he is delusional, how he got into that state, and whether there might be a more realistic approach to the problem. Feelings are explored as we further limit his delusional propensity by our intensive psychotherapeutic exploration and comprehension of his regression to paranoid delusional thinking. George now understands the logical distinction between implication and inference; he sees that he mistakenly thought others implied or intended when it was really his own creative associative inferences to which George was reacting.

Our goal currently is to solidify the gains of an intensive psychodynamic psychotherapy, as George continues to work through explored and unexplored issues that couldn't be kept under wraps previously with high levels of antipsychotics and full-time hospital care. Hopefully we can continue the downward titration of medication, as his stability warrants. This ostensibly "untreatable" patient, after more than ten years of hospitalisation, a quarter century of paranoid psychosis, and the recommendation that he stay in the hospital for life, owes his developing recovery and independence to exploring and understanding his delusions and working them through in the course of a dynamic, insight-oriented outpatient psychotherapy.

Discussion

Regressions to paranoid psychotic modes will probably occur, but they will be approached from the perspective of attempting to help him understand the triggers that lead to intense anxiety and deterioration. George had one several-day hospitalisation while I was on vacation sixteen years ago, and has had other short-lived decompensations not requiring hospitalisation, from which he has learned more about how and why he regresses to a frightened younger self state and paranoia. Psychotic decompensations are treated as opportunities for understanding rather than times to load the patient up with antipsychotics and hospitalise him. For example, earlier in treatment, my vacations led to anger, terror and a sense of abandonment, from which he retreated to a frightened young self who was overwhelmed by paranoia. Gradually he understood that he was regressing to a frightened younger self, feeling abandoned as he had so frequently in early childhood during his parents' vacations. Increasingly, George is aware that there is a moment at which he abdicates rationality and experiences and thinks as a fearful self. His therapeutic task is to catch these transference feelings as they begin and learn to deal with the feelings of anxiety, abandonment and fury, rather than decompsensate.

George was a believer in the adage "any port in a storm". When anxiety came up, he would retreat into a positive delusion (or alcohol) to comfort himself. As a result he ended up with long-standing paranoid beliefs which seemed (but were not) intractable. (He has now abstained from alcohol and drugs for more than a dozen years.) His transference was often that of a cowering, dependent child who needed others to negotiate the world for him, for they had the power. At other times, especially when he was paranoid, his megalomania and grandiose certainty that he was perceiving correctly (in the face of more than a decade of hospitalisation) indicated a strong likelihood that he believed he had a special relationship with God, a surmise he eventually corroborated. At times, in fact, George was certain that he was God.

Countertransference difficulties have been minimal. The main countertransference is that of good parent or protector who enters in and rescues the patient from the throes of a psychotic process which has gone on for so long. When the therapy was strewn with pitfalls and destructive acting out, my conviction that intensive psychotherapy (in conjunction with judicious use of medication) would eventually help stood me in good stead in dealing with any countertransference resentments and frustration.

The question remaining in my mind is why this took so long. Why did this picture persist for so many years, even in excellent treatment settings? Certainly, in a ten-year controlled hospital setting, there was ample opportunity to attempt to help George deal with the underpinnings of his intersecting delusional conclusions. I believe the answer lies in the lack of an attempt to thoroughly understand the patient's disturbance. It is one thing to diagnose and medicate and treat with supportive psychotherapy and social techniques. But if this is not enough, and it certainly was not in George's case, one must unwind the threads that entwine the patient in delusions. The skein, the warp and weft of encircling and debilitating intrapsychic yarn, must be unravelled for clarity to be achieved. I believe that no serious attempt was made to deal with all of George's delusions and the sources of his delusion-making propensity which have been elaborated here. With no comprehensive attempt to decipher the language and meaning of these paranoid schizophrenic productions, George remained what he was when he went into institutions sixteen years before he came to see me: a severely regressed and apparently "untreatable" chronic paranoid schizophrenic.

Perseus' shield of psychodynamic understanding is a powerful tool. In Laing's metaphor, it allows us to enter in and slay the Gorgon of psychosis, if our knowledge is assiduously applied via an intensive psychotherapy. Such is the case even with someone like George, who had been so ill for so long. Why was this method, in conjunction with the judicious use of antipsychotics, not employed in many years in the best treatment settings? I believe it has to do with our field having become convinced that antipsychotic medication is all we can do for severely psychotic patients: at best we can medicate, reality test and help with social adjustments. Furthermore, young psychiatrists have no experience in treating such patients with psychodynamic techniques, and older colleagues (who for the most part have not tried it) doubt that it can be done.

Using George as an example, the attempt to treat him with hospitalisation, medication, social support and reality testing alone proved useless. Only an in-depth exploration and psychotherapeutic working through of his beliefs and the sources of his delusion-making propensity, in conjunction with the judicious use of medication, allowed him first the glimmerings and then the possibility of intrapsychic change and healing. Such an approach allowed George to recognise that all his delusional productions were not messages sent to him by others. He gradually came to recognise that all the paranoid distortions, his belief that television personalities and movie stars and newspapers were in immediate contact with him, were just his own wishes and fears. Such a dynamic, psychotherapeutic approach allowed George to realise that what had caused him such terror and great love was just the result of his own feelings projected onto the external world.

Gradually, this intensive psychodynamic approach led George to the realisation that he was the creator of his own world of psychosis. What he had taken for reality he was now able to see as his own symbolic creation. Little by little, George has begun to recognise his paranoid delusions as his unconscious artistry, not the loving or hostile interest of others. As he has taken on responsibility for his own creativeness, George puts less and less of his beliefs onto others. I only wish that such an approach had been rigorously applied in his previous sixteen years of hospital and institutional care, before he developed enough courage and frustration to leave his hospital care and come to see me and start our journey.

George, previously considered "untreatable" and needing life-long hospitalisation, is a case in progress. Defying Cotswalds' expectations, he is showing increasing independence and an ability to negotiate the world as he has developed an understanding and comprehension of his delusional beliefs. I leave it to the reader to decide which approach is more humane and efficacious in one so disturbed: long-term, perhaps lifelong hospital care as an "untreatable" case or a dynamic outpatient psychotherapy with the chance for healing and cure.

CHAPTER SEVENTEEN

Can anyone that evil ever really die?

Multiple personality, the source of myths about witchcraft, cures by exorcism, and possession by demons, is an oft maligned diagnostic category. Therapists who contend that these patients exist have run into the contempt of their peers, and are often criticised for being gullible and credulous, or for creating iatrogenic disease. Over the last thirty years, it has become a more acceptable diagnosis.

At its most severe, multiple personality disorder is a delusional disorder. Patients believing that they are more than one being must be delusional, believing that they are possessed or just different people at different times. As with the other delusional disorders delineated in this book, multiple personality disorder is amenable to an intensive psychotherapeutic exploration and treatment, as the following case amply demonstrates.

Since the field of multiple personality disorder, its origin and treatment has created so much discussion and question, I refer the reader to Frank Putnam's excellent monograph *Diagnosis and Treatment of Multiple Personality Disorder* (1989) for a more thorough understanding of this disorder. He and I disagree, however, on the usefulness of, or necessity for, hypnosis in the treatment of such patients.

Janet postulated that hysterical symptoms such as amnesia, fugue, conversion symptoms and "successive existences" were a result of patients having split off certain aspects of their personalities, aspects that began to take on a life of their own, with no central unifying ego (Putnam, 1989, p. 2). Janet further demonstrated that these dissociated elements had their origin in past traumatic experiences, and that treatment and change could occur when split off affects and memories were brought into consciousness (Ellenberger, 1970).

Freud and Breuer, in "Studies on Hysteria", wrote that a "double conscience" exists in every hysteria and that the tendency to this dissociation is a fundamental manifestation of this neurosis (1893). The years from 1880 to 1920 were a time of belief in the diagnosis of multiple personality and the presentation of a number of thoroughly researched clinical cases from which various investigators adduced theories about split consciousness and the presence of alter personalities.

With Freud's break with Breuer, and issues on which Masson (1984) has elaborated, Freud began to see hysteria as not necessarily including abnormal states of dissociated consciousness; in addition, he did not regard childhood sexual trauma to be a sine qua non with these patients. Belief in multiple personality declined from 1920 to 1970, with a concurrent increase in the diagnosis of schizophrenia, as opposed to the years from 1914 to 1926, when many more cases of multiple personality than schizophrenia were diagnosed (Rosenbaum, 1980). Questions about the accuracy of the diagnosis, manipulation of therapists by patients, and the possibility that hypnosis furthered the existence of the entity were frequently present in the literature.

In the years since 1970, with the publication of Wilbur's work in *Sybil* (Schreiber, 1973), Bliss and Jeppsen (1985), Kluft (1984) and Putnam (1986a), a number of studies have demonstrated the existence of multiple personality disorder. DSM-III and DSM-IIIR have recognised the existence of such a disorder, classifying it as a Dissociative Disorder or Hysterical Neurosis, Dissociative Type, 300.14. Criteria for this diagnosis are (a) the existence within the personality of two or more distinct personalities or personality states (each with its own relatively enduring pattern of perceiving, relating to, and thinking about the environment and self); and (b) at least two of these personalities or personality states recurrently take full control of the person's behaviour.

In DSM-IV the thrust is that *the patient believes* there are two or more personalities, not that the personalities actually exist. In DSM-IVTR, the following definition applies to Dissociative Identity Disorder: Diagnostic criteria for 300.14 Dissociative Identity Disorder: (a) the presence of two or more distinct identities or personality states (each with its own relatively enduring pattern of perceiving, relating to, and thinking about the environment and self); (b) at least two of these identities or personality states recurrently take control of the person's behaviour; (c) inability to recall important personal information that is too extensive to be explained by ordinary forgetfulness; and (d) the disturbance is not due to the direct physiological effects of a substance.

Clinically, multiple personality can be viewed as childhood dissociation gone wrong. In the NIMH survey of 100 MPD patients (see Putnam et al., 1986), there was nearly always a history of trauma, generally sexual (85%), often violence (75%), extreme neglect (more than 60%), or witnessing a violent death (40%). Dissociation, originally a self-protective mechanism to aid the patient in dealing with an intolerable situation, gradually leads to the patient believing in an actual being or beings, termed alters, who take on split off affects, memories and resultant actions which the patient denies as his or her own. Sometimes the patient is aware of the other personae; often the patient is consciously unaware of them.

Some children, to deal with painful and often repeated abuses, develop imaginary companions; depending on the nature, frequency and severity of the abuse, the imaginary companion may stay as an alter personality, taking on autonomous functions of which the host personality is often ignorant. The host personality wants to be in the dark as to the painful situations he or she is fleeing intrapsychically; it becomes a shell game as to who has any responsibility for behaviour, thoughts and feelings. Amnesia often exists for periods of time; patients report being told they were really different the last time they were seen. Often they make up a history as to how some hours were spent, having no conscious recollection of events. They frequently look different during the course of sessions and will, in the most extreme versions, dress, talk and act differently from their usual modus vivendi. Invariably, they lose time, and don't have an ongoing consistent thread of time and activities. They will switch from one persona to another, often awakening thinking and feeling that they are different; sometimes in sessions, they will look blank or tired for a moment, then switch to another way of being, probably having self-induced a trance and dissociated to another state.

This is the essence of dissociation and its extreme, multiple personality. The patient has learned how to remove him or herself from a noxious situation. Imagine a child being molested, often repeatedly, or physically abused. To deal with the overwhelming stimuli of pain, sexual excitement, anxiety or guilt, the patient may try to ward off feelings. What better way to be gone, to remove oneself from whatever the upsetting circumstance might be, than to hold one's breath, or slow one's breath down in an attempt to diminish powerful, self-annihilating feelings.

Sometimes a traumatised child can stay in the painful traumatising situation; sometimes the child's psyche will contract and retreat inwardly to try to escape such pain; at other times, overwhelmed by fear, he or she will split psychically and be gone from the situation, gone to the belief that he or she is another person to whom the pain is not happening. This patient, tied to a tree overnight, recounted how she wished herself to the moon, focused hard enough and long enough that she was no longer tied standing in the bitter cold, but was another person, happily playing on the moon. Another patient, raped repeatedly for nearly thirty years by her father, tells how she would go off to be another person by intently thinking of happy times and pleasant places; quickly she removed herself from the frightening and stimulating sexual encounter and would find herself with a slightly older, delightful playmate. Together, the two inseparable friends would joke and dance all over the place, paying little or no attention to the much larger man heaving away on top of some other little girl.

Women dissociate and split five times as frequently as men, although Bliss and Larson (1985) raise the possibility that many males who have multiple personality disorder are in the criminal justice system, acting out violently or as sex offenders, rather than in the mental health system. Clinically, these patients often present with a wealth of psychiatric, neurological, and medical symptoms. Frequently, the underlying dissociative process is hidden under a wide variety of complaints as diverse as depression, insomnia, fatigue and terrifying nightmares or hypnopompic and hypnogogic phenomena.

Dissociation may lead to amnesia, fugue episodes, and feelings of depersonalisation (Putnam et al, 1986). Phobic or anxiety symptoms are often present and may be the initial presenting symptoms. "The majority of MPD patients will experience auditory and/or visual hallucinations, though they will seldom admit to these experiences early in therapy" (Putnam, 1989, p. 61). Voices are often critical and berating, may discuss the patient in the third person, and may argue among themselves. Visual hallucinations may occur with changes in the patients' body image when looking in the mirror. Violent scenes, fragments of memories that have been dissociated, and intrusive hideous images frequently occur. Five to twelve percent of patients report tactile and olfactory hallucinations (ibid., p. 62). Sometimes these patients may switch rapidly from one persona or alter to another. Suicidal behaviour and self-mutilation are extremely common. Again from the NIMH study, 14% presented with catatonia (ibid., pp. 62-65), which may have been a way of filtering out or slowing down intolerable stimuli to a tolerable level.

Untreated, the disorder persists over long periods of time, and although it may gradually decrease in intensity, it may shatter the lives of untreated or mistreated patients. One of my patients was still being hospitalised in her late fifties after thirty years of treatment by other psychiatrists, including an incident in her early fifties when one of her personae caused her to jump off the Golden Gate Bridge; luckily another persona grabbed onto a catwalk on the way down, and she pulled herself agonizingly back up to be hospitalised for a number of months with multiple broken bones.

In short, these patients exist; they at any rate believe that there is more than one person in them. They usually explain it as a function of the spirit world, or some strange psychic phenomena. When pressed to account for the other people, they become very vague, and generally will not describe the wealth of different self states they experience until they know the psychiatrist very well. Some will hide what they view as their essential self from the therapist in the hope of continuing an intrapsychic compromise which, though painful, is familiar and affords them the benefit of not really being responsible for their actions. This lack of responsibility is a cardinal feature of such patients. They essentially function like the little kid who has raided the chocolate cake, and when asked about it says: "I didn't do it, Piggy did it." As long as they can continue deceiving themselves, they will.

To accept responsibility for a worsening picture of deceit, lying manipulation, promiscuity, and often criminal acts would be difficult for any of us. For these people, who are often not aware of what they have done but only vaguely remember having lost track of time, such an admission is far more difficult. The lack of a central self responsible for one's acts is motivated by powerful and painful un-integrated affects and memories. To be a central responsible self means coming face to face with these intense phenomena and memories of the painful and traumatic circumstances that led to the dissociation. Since the hurtful, noxious circumstances which led to the dissociation never were worked through, the self, in its various fragments, is experienced as extremely vulnerable. One patient described her inner experience as raw and without a skin; to allow herself to verbalise would lead to air on the exquisitely tender skin, and the fear of shock and death.

Even though these patients believe strongly in the existence of many personalities, I do not believe in it. I believe that they may have numerous autonomous or semi-autonomous self states, dissociated to one degree or another from each other: I view them as physical beings who have dissociated. For example, a forty-year-old woman may view herself in the mirror as a five-year-old child; I view her as a forty-year-old woman trying to run away from herself and also trying to tell us something by regressing to a five-year-old self image. As therapists, our task is to raise questions about the regression, questions as to the meaning of it both currently and as a transference phenomenon.

In the same vein, I don't see a necessity for using hypnosis with these patients. They are highly imaginative, often creative people who need little encouragement to split and fragment themselves still further, as is often the result with hypnosis. Most likely they have many years of experience with self-induced trances, in effect hypnotising themselves. I believe, and have found through clinical experience, that it is possible to search out these personae through the usual intensive psychotherapy, focusing on altered self states, regression from painful memories or affects, and the propensity to dissociate. If one keeps an open mind to the possibility of actual and often horrendous trauma, one can empathically explore and integrate even the most shattered psyche. One might ask why I don't use hypnosis if it can make things clearer and aid the rapidity of integration. My own sense, in reading others' case reports, is that hypnosis provides no benefit in shortening the time of treatment and aiding in integration.

Hypnosis may often lead to iatrogenically induced fantasies and certainties about trauma that never occurred. In fact, I feel it furthers a central difficulty these patients have: it aids them in the avoidance of responsibility for their acts and self states. At the risk of sounding moralistic, hypnosis seems a further infantilisation of these already regressed and self-infantilising patients. To my mind, hypnosis encourages an infantile orientation; the patient for his or her part may respond with increasing self fragments and dissociation rather than regarding the fragments as painful memories, fantasies or affects from which he or she is attempting to flee.

I can't say that my method is definitely faster, but I can demonstrate that it has worked in a number of patients where previous supportive therapies have left the patient either worse or unimproved, still subject to the un-integrated vicissitudes of his or her disorder. I can say that left untreated, or poorly treated with supportive psychotherapy, antipsychotic medication and/or hypnosis, the patient will remain markedly disturbed and prone to the repeated self-distortion and dissociation that led to the disorder in the first place. In-depth, insight-oriented psychotherapy offers the patient not just a chance to develop integrity and responsibility, but a chance for a lasting cure. With hypnosis, there is the possibility of worsening the condition and inducing an iatrogenic disorder; in addition, the literature seems to show a fascination by the hypnotising therapist with the diverse personalities. There seems, at times, to be a competition among hypnotising and reporting therapists to uncover the most personalities possible. Some hypnotising therapists load patients up on all manner of tranquillisers, further diminishing reality testing and enhancing the tendency to blur boundaries.

My orientation is different: it is to point out the central difficulty of trying to flee intrapsychic pain through dissociation, fleeing past and present pain by regressing in the transference to earlier self and imaginary self states. We must remember that these patients are primarily in regressed, transference-ridden states. To my mind, transference and resistance interpretations are paramount with patients suffering from multiple personality disorder, coupled with empathic concern for the likelihood that they have actually gone through painful, abusive experiences as children.

As far as I am concerned, five, ten, twenty, thirty or more personae or personality fragments are unimportant. What is necessary is to get a general road map which will most likely include a history of infantile trauma and dissociation from painful situations to an intrapsychic life with imaginary companions who stay on. Gradually, it will be necessary psychotherapeutically to explore their origin and why they persist. Then it is necessary continually to point out the psychodynamics, to get the patient to be aware of bouncing from self state to regressed self state. The patient is led to monitor him or herself, to become aware of the continually shifting self states, and begins to enquire about why and how these fluctuations in self states happen.

Of course, resistances to such exploration are very likely to occur, since patients believe these self states and imaginary companions and various personae to be real. Gradually, through pointing out, exploring and confronting, as well as seeking the origin of such phenomena, progress will be made. If handled adroitly, the resistance to being one person will be seen as a means of keeping out of consciousness much of the pain that led to such a shattered situation. The thrust is always to regard the patient as a responsible being, and to try and make clear how he or she is attempting to maintain a regressed self state or states in an attempt to flee his or her own life and experience. This integration is accomplished by paying attention to dissociation and the usual parameters of transference, to the existence of the unconscious, and above all to resistance to accepting one's continuity and responsibility as a person. To accept that they are only one person means that they have to acknowledge and integrate the actual pain, rather than clinging to the violated self of the past, and to all those selves created to overcome or escape from perceived and/or experienced trauma.

The major modification necessary in the successful treatment of these patients is to be aware that they may be talking about actual traumatic events, not just fantasies. Often patients try to turn the traumatic experiences around as if it were just their own fetid, highly active imagination, and blame themselves rather than attributing responsibility to another who traumatised them. It is easier for them to blame themselves and become depressed and self-mutilating than to deal with and integrate their fury at those who have actually done them injury. Many patients I have seen have had long courses of psychotherapy of an extremely supportive nature, yet were left in the throes of a pervasive and debilitating disorder. The underlying dissociative process had not been worked on sufficiently in the transference.

Orne (1989) cautions against necessarily believing the memories of hypnosis as being actual events, and further cautions against the therapist calling forth different personae via hypnosis, thereby reifying and concretising the patient's own dramatic intrapsychic mechanisms and excesses. Some proponents of hypnosis regard it as merely creative imagining. To the extent that the patient can become aware that he or she is creating alters, the varying personae and regressed self states, by his or her own symbolising and imaginative functions, this will be helpful. To the extent that the patient views the therapist as the hypnotist who calls forth these phenomena, and does not realise that he or she is the creator of these phenomena, hypnosis will be harmful. Again, the thrust of treatment must be for the patient to integrate his or her life's experiences without retreat to delusional presences.

Freud started out, in "The Aetiology of Hysteria" (1896), viewing these events as actual trauma, and gradually changed his view from the seduction theory to a theory of psychic incestuous wishes. Leaving aside the question of how frequently trauma underlies a less severe psychological disturbance, the dissociative disorders that take on the extreme form of multiple personality disorder are often a reaction to extremely traumatic events. We know this generally from patient accounts or from corroborative evidence of physical abuse, doctors' reports and X-rays, as was the case here. Usually there are no witnesses to these traumatic events, although the spouse may suspect, deny and duck the issue, as happened in this particular case.

Intensive dynamic psychotherapy avoids the pitfalls of credulity on the part of the therapist and iatrogenic distortions via hypnosis. Intensive, insight-oriented work allows the patient to reintegrate and achieve responsibility for his or her own life through our familiar use of interpretation regarding flight from pain through dissociation, and interpretation of resistance against accepting one's solitary, frightened nature in a painful past and current transference-ridden situation. Even in the most severe disturbance, often caused by a reaction to heinous circumstances in childhood, delusions may be worked through and eradicated where previous treatment has left the patient fragmented and regressed. The following case will demonstrate the usefulness of such an insight-oriented approach in the treatment of one so disturbed and delusional.

Clinical case of multiple personality disorder

This case was published by the patient under a pseudonym as *Broken Child* (Cameron, 1995). I refer the reader to it for an in-depth personal account of the pain of a delusional disorder, its myriad destructive ramifications and eventual successful and healing treatment.

Marcia is a 55-year-old mother of two, with a lifetime history of dissociative disorder; by the age of five she was already a multiple personality. She is the second child and only daughter in a family of three children; she has a brother two years older and one a year younger. The mother was a psychotic, frequently hallucinating woman who saw evil in her daughter and attempted to exorcise this evil by repeated tortures. The father was a successful professional man who knew of the mother's abuse, but did nothing until much too late.

When she first came in nearly twenty years ago, Marcia was profoundly suicidal and frantic, having just been abruptly terminated by her second psychiatrist, whom she had been seeing for 18 months. (Her first psychotherapy had lasted two and a half years in another location.) The second psychiatrist had found it impossible to maintain his boundaries with her, since she would call and leave messages on his machine threatening his children. She had become convinced that he was treating her sadistically, as had her mother. Rather than interpreting the transference, by both his and Marcia's account he became increasingly quiet—she said he was a very good and sensitive listener—and was mistakenly and transferentially seen by her as hostile and torturing. The situation between them worsened in an apparent transference-countertransference dilemma which he resolved not by interpretation, but by seeking consultation, and on the consultant's recommendation abruptly ending Marcia's therapy. Obviously, a period of time should have been included in such a course of action, but he felt under the gun and overwhelmed by her productions. In short, he and the consultant reacted by removing him physically from the patient, just as the patient had removed herself intrapsychically from painful and overwhelming situations via dissociation.

In his defence, the psychiatrist told me that Marcia had called and left a message on his home machine as "Sunshine", threatening harm to him and his family, and it was this that led him to such a precipitous course. Marcia had to deal not only with her usual troubles but with the pain of abandonment by her therapist with whom she had been intensely involved. There had been an all or nothing split in her view of him. For a number of months he had been the all good, ostensibly protective father, just like the one she pretended to herself she had had while growing up. When, after more than a year, she began to project onto him the anticipated evil she had experienced at the hands of her mother, it came without warning and was not dealt with by psychological means due to the dissociated and apparently uncharacteristic fury of her interaction with her therapist. Too bad, for the themes of all good, all bad, anticipated sadism and murderous rage were all grist for the therapeutic mill.

By a rather circuitous route, Marcia was referred to me by a third psychiatrist who had been the administrative and medicine dispensing psychiatrist while the second psychiatrist was engaged in her psychotherapy. He had tried varying doses and types of medicine, including antipsychotic medicines, but with little ameliorative effect: Marcia became increasingly fragmented and suicidal during the course of psychotherapy. Parenthetically, in addition to nearly always making interpretations to these patients about both the dissociative process and the extent of their productions, thereby offering them a container for their difficulties, I believe it is a bad idea to have an administrator-therapist split in patients who do so much splitting on their own. I prefer to keep all the splitting phenomena in my own purview, all the better to interpret them to the patient.

Marcia's story emerged in fits and starts: a shard here, a vignette there. When she first came in, she was an unkempt, volatile, tearful woman. Not only was she profoundly suicidal and threatening to end her life, she could only afford a quarter of my usual fee. I debated internally for a few moments as to whether I even wanted to deal with a person with such difficulties and lack of funds for both treatment and hospital backup, if necessary. She felt profoundly suicidal, and had previously made a number of suicide attempts. I could tell during that first session that she would be chaotic and deeply disturbed, and recognised immediately that she was a person suffering from a very severe example of multiple personality disorder. I knew she could not adhere to any contracts she made with me not to harm herself.

My thought process went something like this: She's going to be very difficult. There is something very appealing about this woman. She's in extremely dire straits in every way. She's very likely to kill herself if I don't see her (hopefully not too grandiose a thought on my part). She has suffered tremendously and doesn't even know it. In short, she is likely to get worse before she has a chance to improve. She has seen a number of psychiatrists since the abrupt termination of her therapy, and for various reasons no one will see her as a patient. If I don't help her, she is not likely to get any help, since she is threatening to go to the Bridge today (again, hopefully accurate and not too grandiose). She is unlikely to get to a hospital, and if I call the police to hospitalise her involuntarily for a day or two, she'll just get out of the county hospital. The upshot of my ruminations and assessment during Marcia's first session was that I decided to see her. My reasoning was pretty much as I've described: I just had a sense that she would kill herself if I didn't see her—she had been referred to me as a last resort. So with that kind of billing, why not see her?

It was a gamble that paid off. Even though Marcia was often suicidal, she never acted on these suicidal impulses during the course of an intensive psychotherapy which revealed layer upon layer of both physical and psychological trauma and their effects on her developing psyche. On a number of occasions there were close calls. Once "Joey", a sixteen-year-old angry boy took over, telling me he had bought bullets for her husband's gun. (At my urging, Marcia gave me the bullets.) In another instance, she came to with a large quantity of rat poison that "Sunshine" and "Joey" had made her buy. Throughout it all, however, she was able to contact me, either directly or through some split off guiding aspect, before she could fulfil her desire to be dead.

Let's get back to her story. Marcia had consulted her first psychiatrist in her early forties for depression, shortly after she had thrown herself down a very long flight of concrete stairs in a suicide attempt. She had thrown herself down the stairs at the incessant urging of one of her delusional presences, which kept hectoring her to kill herself. She tried to resist, but eventually gave in to the incessant clamouring for her death from a delusional being which appeared to her to be outside herself. No one realised, and she didn't say, that it was a suicide attempt; she said that she had stumbled and fallen.

Patients like Marcia hardly ever come in complaining of many different personalities, generally not being conscious of them. Even if they are conscious of the different delusional personae, it often takes a considerable period of time for the patient to trust the therapist enough to tell him. The therapist for his or her part must keep a mind open to the possibility of dissociative disorder leading to a lack of continuity of history if there are blackouts, inexplicable events in the history, amnesia or fugue states.

Gradually, during the time of Marcia's first therapy, she became aware of a long-standing promiscuity and kleptomania. As far as she was concerned, this was not her: it was "Jennifer". The patient would forget hours or days, and realise later that she had stolen things, or spent the night with a strange man. Slowly, she realised that she would go off to be "Jennifer" whenever she had difficulty at home or was bored or upset by something. She remembered that she had gone off to be "Jennifer" when she was three to escape from her mother's abuse. "Jennifer", who had allegedly died during the first therapy (she came back during ours), remembered the history the patient had done her best to forget. "Jennifer" was very angry at what had been done to her, and tried to protect Marcia.

Once I heard about "Jennifer" surfacing and ostensibly dying during Marcia's first therapy, I began asking questions about "Jennifer's" origin. Little by little, the history Marcia had tried to forget came out as told by this delusional presence, "Jennifer", who was Marcia pretending to herself that she was "Jennifer". Marcia pretended because she was attempting to avoid intrapsychically the pain of the experiences which led to the dissociative and delusional formation of "Jennifer". "Jennifer's" history, which was corroborated to a great extent through physical examination by Marcia's internist, and also by the family, was as follows:

Marcia's mother was a Germanic, psychotic woman with strong Nazi sympathies, who had a number of psychiatric hospitalisations, two during the first three years of Marcia's life. Her father was a Jewish attorney who was extremely successful and promiscuous.

The mother hated Jews in general, and her daughter (who looked like her father) in particular. The mother often hallucinated, talking to angels and devils, as Marcia recalls. She threatened repeatedly to send Marcia away with the gypsies, who would do even more terrible things to her than her mother did if Marcia ever told what her mother did to her. At times, nurses and housekeepers were in the house when the mother was most disturbed, but not for long enough to protect Marcia from the torture and mutilation her mother began to inflict on her.

Over the years of therapy, further historical information surfaced. The mother may have been seduced by her own father for a two-year period in adolescence. In addition, the mother's mother may have been sexually involved with her son-in-law (Marcia's father) at the time of Marcia's birth; at least that's what Marcia's mother thought. This belief and the father's philandering may have played a part in Marcia's mother's psychotic decompensations. Two hospitalisations and shock treatment for the mother in the first three years of Marcia's life compounded the mother's difficulties, as did a probable sexual relationship between the mother and the mother's psychiatrist, by the patient's eventual account. Needless to say, there was a great deal disturbing Marcia's mother, who regarded Marcia as primarily her father's child, and appears to have taken out much of her hatred for her husband on Marcia, the "Jewish child" who looked like her husband.

When Marcia was four, her mother began to lock her in a closet for hours on end—no food; no facilities. "Jennifer" began as Marcia's attempt to leave the situation. While Marcia was alone and terrified in the dark closet, "Jennifer" would go outside to play. As the abuse continued, Marcia became "Jennifer" more and more frequently, no longer suffering the pain inflicted on her as Marcia. She would focus really intently on being somewhere else, and suddenly she would be out of the situation she was in.

Marcia described the process of dissociation in a vignette from the age of eight, but the same process pertains at any age. She is with her family at a cabin by a lake in the woods. The father returns to work, leaving the psychotic mother with the children. The mother picks out her favourite victim, Marcia, and ties her to a tree. The tree cuts into her body; ants and bugs crawl all over her. The mother tells her that bears will come and eat her in the night, and leaves her. The other

children are too terrified, as a result of a lifetime of the mother's intimi-
dation and brutality, to help her. To escape the cold, the pain and her
fear, Marcia focuses on the moon, wishing as hard as she can that she
were on the moon. Suddenly she is on the moon, playing to her heart's
content with the man in the moon. By the time her mother unties her
bonds the next morning, she has no memories of the terrors of the
night, only the marks of the rope on her body. Clearly the dissociation
had a beneficial effect, protecting her from the full realisation of her
situation with her mother, but at a terrible cost.

Incidents of abuse by the mother when Marcia was in second grade
alone included numerous finger fractures with nutcrackers, concus-
sion, broken arms, and many contusions. Marcia's mother would
use different doctors each time so that no one would get too clear
a picture. Marcia recalls the school principal coming to her house
when she was in third grade and asking her in front of both parents if
anyone was hurting her. Fearing the mother, Marcia said no one hurt
her. Afterwards there was a fight between her parents. Marcia hoped
her father would take her away, but he just packed his bags and left
as he always did, on pretence of business, leaving Marcia with her
mother. She wished he were protective; he knew, but did little or
nothing to safeguard her. Repeatedly, teachers would ask Marcia if
there was any trouble at home, but as she feared being given away
to the gypsies—and what the gypsies would do to her—even more
than she feared her mother, she always said no.

Other incidents of abuse recalled by Marcia include, when she
was five, her mother sticking a knife point into her repeatedly, tying
her by all extremities to a bed and masturbating her, at the same time
telling her daughter that she was evil. Once, at the age of five, Marcia
hit her mother back; she was tied up again, and had her labia sewn
shut for several hours. (Reconstructive surgery to her vaginal area in
her twenties indicated that something had been done to her, but she
had no memory as to what. At the time of the surgery she exhibited
the bland indifference characteristic of hysterics. Bland indifference,
of course, is just a defence against self-awareness and a consistent
self-recollection.) Pet animals were slaughtered: cats, dogs and goats
killed by knife, bat and car; aquarium fish were boiled alive.

Here is another example of the mother at work. When Marcia was
eleven, the mother uncharacteristically urged the children to have a
Halloween party and invite other kids. Marcia was suspicious, since

her mother rarely let other kids come over, but gradually got into the spirit of the party. The mother even suggested a game of everybody putting their fingers into a bowl of jelly and marshmallows, to pretend they were putting their hands into a ghoulish mix. Marcia recalled going out with her mother to get marshmallows, and making the concoction with her mother, who was in an unusually good mood. During the Halloween party the mother switched bowls; the lights were turned on after everybody had dipped their hands into the bowl, presenting them with the ghastly picture of blood dripping all over the kids, for the bowl now contained cows' eyes swimming around in cows' blood. Needless to say, the party broke up abruptly, and Marcia and the other children became increasingly outcast at school.

At the age of eight, Marcia broke a leg trying to fly from a rooftop. She was trying to fly to God, for God would protect her. In her late thirties, when she threw herself down a flight of stairs, she was trying to kill herself at the urging of one of her destructive delusional personae, resulting in many broken bones and a long convalescence in the hospital. Suicidal thoughts were often with her.

There were numerous terrible events. One Easter time, while her father was away on one of his trips, Marcia was hung up on a balcony, like Christ. The mother, uttering imprecations and talking visibly to her angel, plunged a poker into Marcia, as the symbolic Jew and hated representative of her father. Marcia was eventually cut down and taken to the hospital, where she was sutured and kept in for several days. When the father realised what had happened, there was a housekeeper in the house for several months, but according to Marcia, the housekeeper was more concerned about her job than about Marcia's safety.

On another occasion, the mother had the children dig a hole in the back yard, after Marcia—at the age of eleven—had yelled back at her mother and tried to hit her. Marcia was forced to lie in the hole overnight, covered with dirt, straining for breath, for all but her face was covered. Again, the father was away and the mother hallucinating. When her siblings protested, they were hit and sent crying to their rooms. Marcia feared that worms or snakes would enter her in the night and that she would die there. Of course, she was so terrified that she dissociated and wasn't there after a while. In the morning she came to as her older brother mustered up enough courage to dig her out. Again she didn't report this to anyone.

One might ask: are these events true, or not true? At the very least they were a psychic reality to her and seemed real to me in the telling. One of her siblings has read her book and has sent me a letter stating that the events were so. It seems so horrible to do such things to a child that I will not insist on their veracity, though they seem likely enough to me. I leave it to the reader to separate out actual events from psychological reality, if that is an important issue.

Marcia remembered another occasion when, at the age of eleven, she wanted to kill her mother for all the abuse. For several minutes, she stood with a gun pointing at her mother as she slept, thinking of killing her mother and then herself. The mother awakened, slapped her and took the gun away.

Marcia's anger at her mother was beginning to escalate as she approached puberty. This could have been a sign of health, but understandably she couldn't contain it in one person. Her totally reasonable (although murderous) fury was deposited in yet another delusional persona.

According to Marcia, her father saw but ignored blood in her knickers after her mother sewed her labia; he considered Marcia to be "accident-prone". He might create a little fuss, but would always leave her in her mother's care while away either on business trips or with other women. By all accounts, he saw many different women as he tried to cope with an often hallucinating and disturbed wife. Such manoeuvres undoubtedly made his wife even more disturbed and heightened the pressures on Marcia. Finally, the increasing hospital visits, broken bones and scars forced her father to ask her, when she was twelve, if anything was wrong. Even though she still feared what would happen to her if she was given to the gypsies, she told him the truth. No longer able to deny the reality of what he must have suspected, he grabbed the children and moved away from the mother.

Marcia was so happy; her terror began to abate. For nearly two years the four of them lived happily together. The physical and emotional scars began to recede. She and her brothers would play on the beach, enjoyed a new school, and finally sensed some security as the father spent a great deal of time with them. There were no visits to the mother.

When Marcia was fourteen, her father died in a plane crash. The children were returned to their mother as no arrangements had been made for them to be placed with relatives or social services. There had been a supportive bond between the children, but the older brother immediately ran away, leaving Marcia to bear the brunt of her mother's rage. Luckily, her mother had to take in boarders to make ends meet, so the tortures were less frequent. Marcia lived in constant terror of her mother, frequently dissociating into more and more beings. For many years afterwards, Marcia was convinced that through a bomb or evil telepathy her mother had caused her father's plane to crash. In therapy she recovered the memory of the state troopers coming to the door with pictures of the crash, and seeing one with her father's flannel shirt and "no face". Her grief as she uncovered this sequestered painful event was overwhelming.

At seventeen Marcia had encephalitis and was hospitalised for a number of months, during which time—as all too often happens to these repeatedly victimised people—she was raped repeatedly by an orderly. After several months he was apprehended; unsurprisingly, the patient had been too terrorised to tell, just as she'd been too terrified of the gypsies to tell of her mother's abuse. Even though Marcia wasn't fully recovered and couldn't walk, her mother insisted she be signed out of the rehabilitation hospital against medical advice. Her mother locked Marcia, already weak, in a room where she was unable to get out of bed. When her younger brother finally mustered the courage to call the authorities, after the mother had repeatedly beaten him and threatened to kill him, Marcia was found in an emaciated, dehydrated, befouled state. Finally, social services got into the act and the children were taken away from their mother.

Even though Marcia was free of her mother physically, she was easily victimised by others. She was raped on a number of occasions, and often got into sadomasochistic relationships. She would be looking for a protective father; they would be looking for a quick roll in the hay or a woman to control. In her mid-twenties she married a quiet, loving, non-demonstrative slightly older man. He unfortunately never asked about her being out at nights, and never confronted her about the bizarreness that occurs when one dissociates to other personalities.

As we pieced together her history, listening over a number of chaotic sessions to "Jennifer's" tale, Marcia realised that a number of delusional personae developed over the years, seven in all. Having once dissociated from being Marcia at the age of four to being the playful little girl "Jennifer", it was a simple matter for Marcia to continue the process of dissociation and subsequently create other beings. This isn't surprising, since human inventiveness is manifold. If she could invent one persona at four, a persona which gradually became concretised into "Jennifer", a delusional being she believed in, it was a simple matter to invent other delusional presences which increasingly took on a life of their own. Soon they seemed to be discrete persons, sometimes communicating with the others, often having different functions, and often at cross purposes with each other.

In addition to Marcia, the "host" personality and "Jennifer", there were five delusional others which she believed to exist somehow, in some way, within her. She thought they were all people, perhaps put there spiritually, or maybe she was possessed. Perhaps they all coexisted within one body—at times she would look younger or older to herself in the mirror. Most probably she didn't think about the different people she believed herself to be in an analytic fashion at all.

There was "Camille", a sickly personality alternating between a little girl of six or seven and a teenager, crying, fearful, just wanting help and comfort. "Camille" would come up when Marcia felt frightened or needy. As "Camille", she practised for the time her mother would blind her with an ice-pick, coding her clothes in the closet in some form of Braille fashion, so that when she was blinded she could dress herself. As "Camille" she anticipated being hurt, and prepared for this eventuality.

"Sophie" was a warm, comforting woman in her sixties, rather like Marcia's Jewish grandmother, who just happened to have been named Sophie and had been the one warm and constant person in Marcia's life until she died when Marcia was twelve. "Sophie" often comforted "Camille" or Marcia and played with "Jennifer". When Marcia baked cookies or played with her children, it was not Marcia but "Sophie" who did these things. It would have been one thing for Marcia to pretend she was being like her grandmother when she baked; it was quite another to actually believe with certainty that it was "Sophie" who did the baking.

Again, even though people suffering from multiple personality disorder are often quite intelligent, they are also incredibly naive and unaware when it comes to understanding the symbolism or origin of each of their personalities. More precisely, since they are delusional and view these personae as real beings, they have a definite interest in not asking questions and in remaining vague and confused about the different people and what they mean. Feelings, fantasies, and metaphor are treated as concrete, reified beings. These patients remain unconscious of having created their own delusional beings, due to a mix of repression, indifference, wish fulfilment and self-distraction, in an attempt to shield themselves from the very real pain they are experiencing.

Then there was "Joey", an angry 16-year-old boy wanting revenge on those who had injured Marcia; alternatively, "Joey" was so filled with rage that he wanted to kill Marcia. It was "Joey" who had bought the bullets and the rat poison and threatened to kill her; it was "Joey" who threw her down the flight of stairs when she made the suicide attempt in her thirties. For years "Joey" acted violently and impulsively, stealing and urging Marcia or others to hop in bed with one guy or another. At times he helped Marcia, defending and supporting her as her older brother had. More frequently "Joey" was a destructive personality, raging at Marcia's mother for all the sadistic things she had done and at her father for being too weak to help and protect her. Until we began to explore "Joey", Marcia hadn't realised the obvious, that "Joey" was the age her brother was when he left her with her mother. She had clung to him in her psychic life as an adolescent, angry male personality. Wasn't he somewhat protective? Weren't girls more seriously abused by her mother then boys?

"Sunshine" was a needy and angry child who began at age five, and tried to comfort the even more terrified Marcia, and sometimes played with "Jennifer". "Sunshine" was the one who frightened away the second psychiatrist by threatening his family. "Sunshine" joined forces with "Joey" to urge promiscuous, antisocial behaviour.

"Muriel" was an artist from Tasmania whose parents were very well off; she loved the arts and an elegant, bohemian lifestyle. How she came from Tasmania was a mystery, as was anything that occurred prior to the age of 23, when she had begun in Marcia's life. "Muriel" was an idealised self, competent, able, intelligent and seductive, who appeared as Marcia tried to make a life for herself shortly before she got married.

All of these personalities, in my retelling of them, sound rather hollow and trite; to a great extent they were to me. To Marcia, however, they were reality, filled with a vitality and depth I am unable to express accurately, if only because I see them as drama meant to distract her from her essential terrified, lonely, and brutalised self. She believes in them, hence vivifies the dissociated and delusional aspects of her being with no perspective. To her, there are seven persons inhabiting one body; accordingly, the drama mounts logarithmically.

The first therapist only gradually realised that the patient was dissociated, and let the material emerge. Generally this is a good idea, but with people so disturbed it is imperative that an intellectual container focusing on reality testing, genetic reconstruction and transference interpretations be constructed. Neither of the previous therapists did this, and they foundered between the Scylla of empathy and the Charybdis of non-intervention.

Severely dissociative and delusional people like Marcia need not just understanding but containment through reality testing and interpretation regarding the origin of their numerous personalities. Such an approach is bound to make them worse in the short run, for they are tenaciously clinging to the delusional belief that the projected parts are not self. First the patient must be made to realise how disturbed he or she is. I don't mince words and tell the patient in whatever way is necessary, using whatever art of psychotherapy I possess, that he or she is dissociative or delusional, or highly imaginative—sometimes the shock value of the statement gets the patient's attention. At the same time I explain the dissociative process, the origin of the delusional personality, and try to get across an understanding that the patient's need to escape a psychologically (and often physically) painful life experience is responsible for his or her belief in multiple personalities.

There is no hard and fast rule as to when to begin the interpretive confrontation with the patient's view of things. Using this patient as an example, a period of two or three months of empathically gathering a history replete with examples of dissociation is more than adequate to get the broad outlines. Instead, Marcia had had four years of becoming increasingly disturbed while the other two therapists sensitively listened, understood, and (I assume) made some comments that were empathic. I increased the pressure on her after several months—as far as I was concerned, enough was enough. The process was clear to me; now to make it clear to her.

During this time I was available for additional appointments, or by telephone, and used a little antipsychotic medication—though never as much as Marcia had taken during her previous therapy. Such an approach gradually helped Marcia reality test and go through the inevitable suicidal feelings, humiliation at having wasted so much time, fury at those who had traumatised her, and sadness at having made such a terrible mess of her life. As the anger is mobilised, there may be some suicidal thought, but no multiple personality I have treated in this way has made a serious suicide attempt at this point. I think they are enmeshed in the therapeutic process, and are carried along towards fusion, integration and health. The stakes are high, as are both the drama and the noise level, but well worth it for the patient. Perhaps they sense that there is a genuine interest in them, as well as the chance for change. So they persevere rather than ending their lives.

The first therapist gradually realised the extent of the mother's pathology when the mother began to send Marcia knives and guns for birthday and Christmas presents, to some extent corroborating Marcia's account of her treatment at her mother's hands. A number of years ago, Marcia confronted her mother in a burst of anger about the gifts and the message to kill herself with the knives and guns, and took her to task for her sadistic treatment over the years. The mother denied that she had done anything. Marcia's brothers agreed that her account was accurate, but wished she would leave it in the past. About a year later, the mother killed herself. Parenthetically, I've seen another situation where the perpetrator of two years of child abuse abruptly killed himself: perhaps there is a moment of lucidity as to the enormity of their crimes.

Some events in therapy highlight both Marcia's progress and my way of working with such a disturbed patient. After our first year of therapy, in which she had been doing increasingly well, without going off to any of her personalities for two months, I announced that I would be away for three weeks in a month's time. She became terribly fearful, began to cry, and seemed to regress quickly. Soon she was feeling abandoned, feeling like "Camille" at times, certain she was "Sunshine" at others. She was hurt by the abandonment and angry, certain that I would die and never return. My interpretations centred on her transference apprehension being rooted in her father's death in a plane crash and her certainty that even though her mother had been dead for several years, she would be unprotected and vulnerable as she had been with her mother when her father had died.

Between sessions, she called several times, once in a small girl's voice, crying and distraught. Later there was a message from an angry, screaming adolescent, "Joey". Still later there was a call from

"Muriel" telling me what was happening to the poor little girl; then later still some words of advice from "Sophie" as to how to handle the situation. I listened, empathised, and interpreted the splitting and dissociation from her own anger at me for leaving, and pointed out the various transference regressions in the face of her certainty that I would die like her father. I continued to point out her trick of believing that she was one or another delusional person, in order to evade feeling like a frightened little girl.

Little by little she began saying to herself what I had been saying to her, and regressed less frequently to a damaged and abandoned self. I encouraged Marcia to do for herself what I had done for her, to bring herself back by monitoring and interpretation to be one person feeling the pain she had previously tried to escape via dissociation. Of course it would be difficult during my absence, so I arranged for her to see a colleague if necessary, and told her that should I die and not return, he knew her case and would continue working with her; she was not going to be abandoned as she had been previously.

The vacation was difficult for her, and she handled it with fear but no dissociation to other personalities. She heard them talking, but most of the time she was able to talk herself through the situations. She became increasingly angry as she remembered her father's neglect of her and his acquiescence in her mother's brutality. Marcia (not "Joey") became infuriated and stabbed herself once in the leg with an ice pick; it hurt a lot, so she stopped. Previously, had she dissociated to another personality, she could have stabbed herself many times, or mutilated herself in one of the many other ways she had done. This was definite progress. I told her so when I returned, and again pointed out the need to monitor herself and realise that all the others were just an attempt to escape pain, a pain which she unwittingly furthered by believing in her delusional beings. She had kept alive a transference sense that torture and pain at her mother's hands still existed in the form of a painful external reality analogous to her persecutory mother.

Marcia's fear had been that I (the father) would die, leaving her in the hands of an overwhelming reality (the mother), as had happened before. Several more interpretations of the transference nature of her regressions were made in the face of her increasingly dramatic protests that she couldn't get along without the different people. Shortly afterwards, Marcia called, sounding terrified: "They're dying;

I hear their dying breaths; all of them are leaving; I'm terribly fright-ened!" I told her that this was great news and just what I expected; furthermore, her fear was entirely understandable, for she was a frightened child so many years ago when she had to dissociate from all that pain. Now her imaginary friends, the delusional personali-ties were no longer necessary and she would have to become familiar with that underlying frightened aspect of her own being.

Marcia had a lot of apprehension. I told her that she would not die; she was just recognising her basic being, without the artifice and self-deception of believing that there were others there for protec-tion. The best protection was to be armed with reason, I went on; she could now look after her own self and could call me back later that evening. She did. The delusional others were gone. She heard no voices, only her own thoughts. "I need to depend on you for a while; I'm truly alone." I reassured her that I was there with her, and that the situation was quite different from her childhood, when she was actually terrified with good cause and had no one she could turn to for protection.

For several weeks, Marcia was both frightened and very lonely. She missed her others, grieving for them. Her terror was understood as her regression back to the frightened little girl she was before the friends were created. But she remained terrified. Gradually it became clear that Marcia and her brothers all believed that their mother was much more dangerous now that she was dead. At least when she was alive they all knew where she was; now that she was dead, they feared that she had become an all-pervasive evil spirit who could attack any or all of them whenever she wanted. "Can anyone that evil really die?" I reassured her that her mother was dead and that the recent black presence she had seen enveloping her was similar to her delusional creation of other people: this time she had recre-ated her terrorising, angry, punitive mother in concrete, delusional, palpable form. She was alone, terrorised only by her traumatic recol-lections of her mother's evil nature.

In the next session, as we talked more about the mother being dead and unable to harm her, Marcia looked terrified and protested that her mother was right there in her chair. She jumped up and ran across the room to another chair, from which she told me that the mother was still sitting in the first chair. Marcia was screaming, crying and acting terrified; but to her it seemed real. I first told Marcia that this was her own delusion, that she was reacting to her own holographic creation of her mother. I saw no evil spirit; there was none in generally agreed reality, just an increasingly upset Marcia thrashing around my office for no reason other than her reaction to her delusional belief in her evil mother's presence. My reality testing had as much effect on her as spitting in the wind. Marcia escalated her histrionic panic, shrieking and falling to the ground in the face of alleged attacks by the evil spirit of her mother. I decided that a different tack might do the trick.

Quick as I could, I jumped up and reached out, clenched my fist and asked: "Do I have her?" "No, there!" I tried again, and on the third try apparently got the patient's notion of her mother's evil spirit in my fist. Knowing full well that I was playing out an exorcism in Marcia's mind, I told her that she had always wanted someone to stand up to her mother for her. Marcia, gleeful and tearful, told me to lock her up. I rummaged in a drawer, found an old cookie tin, and enclosed her fantasised spirit in it, all the while telling Marcia that we were play acting putting away her mother's evil spirit in a tin. "As far as I am concerned, and if anyone else were watching," I told Marcia, "there is no evil spirit of your mother." I told Marcia that this was just a way to calm her, for there was no evil spirit in the room, only Marcia's concretised fear of her mother.

Marcia was elated: someone had finally taken her side against her mother, even an imaginary, delusional one. We discussed the transference aspects of her fear of her mother, which led her to believe that there was an evil spirit of her mother living on after death and persecuting her as her mother had tortured her in life. In addition, we talked of her lifelong desire that someone should finally stand up to her mother, her transference wish that someone else would deal with her mother, and about the countertransference aspects of my role-playing a protective person dealing with her mother's delusional presence.

Gradually Marcia became increasingly stronger, until her younger brother called on her mother's birthday, to scream and yell at her as the mother would have, telling Marcia that she was responsible for the mother's death. She spent several days crying. A number of interpretations to the effect that she was regressing again to the frightened child, victimised by the mother in the guise of the brother, finally had the desired result. She called her brother, told him how angry she was, and that he should get professional help. She did it herself, not asking anyone else to stand up for her.

Several more weeks of two steps forward and one step back followed. Marcia made increasing strides towards realising that her mother was dead, then regressed to a cowering, terrified little child, wanting above all else to be free of the all-pervading, concretised presence which was the delusional evil spirit of her mother. She became angry at me for having left her without the ability to dissociate to escape her pain and terror. At times she became seriously suicidal for days on end.

My interpretations centred on her frantic attempts to escape her unity. Previously, when frightened by anything that smacked of the evil of her mother, she would regress to a frightened four-year-old and then dissociate to one of the many others. Now she was stuck with no outlet. Suicide appealed to her, but was countered by my describing her psychological processes of regression and flight in an attempt to escape delusional transference situations which were perceived as life-threatening. She had to understand first of all that she was believing in a delusional presence, this time that of her dead mother's ghost. Now she was trying to flee as a regressed self, cowering and fearing the attacks of an all-powerful and overwhelming, torturing mother she believed was there. Suicide was like dissociation: just another way of fleeing. Over a four-week period this interpretation was repeated often enough, and calmly enough, until I began to hear my words coming back to me from Marcia. Whether or not she had gained insight, she had ingested my comforting (and hopefully accurate) comments until they had a chance to become part of her psychic structure. Harsh, intimidating superego was replaced by a developing tolerant, positive superego attribute.

Further examples of therapy

Marcia seemed to be all right for a while; her sense of fragility and disorganisation diminished for a month or so. But in one so disturbed, I knew this was most likely the calm before the storm—more precisely, the first of many calms before many storms. It was a very curious phenomenon. She would have periods of lucidity, calmness and clarity lasting four to eight weeks. Then she would begin to be

CAN ANYONE THAT EVIL EVER REALLY DIE?   171

sleepless, start to hallucinate, and become more childlike, regressed and terrified. Her franticness would escalate, suicidal ideas would increase, and she would deteriorate markedly for anywhere from two to six weeks.

Thinking there might be some cyclical component to these out-bursts, akin to kindling, I tried every mood stabiliser, major and minor tranquilliser possible. She could tolerate none of them, new or old line, due to the upsurge of neuromuscular symptoms which became debilitating. (She also had a tentative diagnosis of lupus or multiple sclerosis from a neurologist.) At best, she might tolerate a very low dose of antipsychotic medicine for a few days, to knock down some of the most severe suicidal and decompensating frenzy.

At these times, Marcia appeared to be hallucinating and extremely regressed, acting like a terrified child. Transference interpretations regarding her bringing up for our inspection the terror and frenzy she had felt as a child were the most helpful. These frantic episodes diminished only when the material that was driving her to frenzy emerged. I told her repeatedly that although these were incredibly stressful events, they were most likely her way of telling us some-thing. Hospitalisation was always available, but never necessary, as she uncovered a series of painful psychological and physically trau-matic memories.

Marcia also was at risk during these times of killing herself, not as Marcia, but as her evil mother killing her. This is strange to contem-plate, but since she was so fragmented and dissociative, it seemed to me that she most probably had a concretised harsh, punitive and delusional presence of her mother, who hated her "Jewish child". Much of her disturbance was driven by believing that knives were moving around at night, placed by an unknown hand. Obviously it was Marcia's own hand, but she claimed to have no knowledge of going to the kitchen and getting knives and placing them in various places in her bedroom. Here's how it worked. Her mother, as men-tioned previously, used to send Marcia knives and guns as gifts. The understood message was: kill yourself. In her regressed state, she would awaken with kitchen knives scattered all over the bedroom. Of course she didn't remember moving them from the kitchen.

Before we began to talk about this, a pattern that had been going on for decades, she believed her mother was actually planting the knives (or ashes in her shoes to say: "Incinerate yourself, Jew") both during her life and as a powerful evil spirit after her death. This form of delusional belief was deeply convincing to Marcia and only diminished over the next several years as a number of profound and hitherto overwhelming psychological events and (as seemed most likely to me) memories surfaced.

To safeguard Marcia from harm to herself, since she would hardly ever alert her husband to what was going on, a number of devices had to be used. A hook was put on her bedroom door, the idea being that this would prevent her from walking into the kitchen to get knives. But first I had to convince her (and I only convinced a small portion of her) that she was the one bringing the knives and ashes into the bedroom. Of course, knives continued to appear in the bedroom. She became increasingly certain that her dead mother was pursuing her, until I explained that she must be unhooking the door or not latching it at all. Then a bell was tied to her leg, so that if she started walking, she might awaken herself.

Whether or not any of these devices worked is questionable. What they did offer, though, was the sense that there might be an alternative explanation to the delusional certainty that her mother was pursuing her from beyond the grave. With a slight inroad made into that delusional belief, some therapeutic work could ensue as her franticness abated somewhat. I told her that we would be able to make sense of these repeated episodes, and gradually we did. I certainly couldn't predict what was about to come up, but had the sense that previously split off and profound material was soon to emerge. Then, following Marcia's lead as she recounted one horrendous event after another, each complete in itself, I could listen empathically and gradually help her through her morass of distortion, fragmentation, powerful affects and memories. I will go into some of these events at greater length, but the pattern was the same for all of them. Each time Marcia would become increasingly frantic, scream and act terrified. Slowly, over weeks, the underlying material would emerge, usually in the office, sometimes not.

In the office, Marcia recalled being hung up like Jesus at Easter time, and having her side pierced with a poker. Her mother dragged her upstairs to the balcony, tied her to the railing, and while hallucinating and talking gibberish about "Our Lord" and "sacrificing Jews", plunged a poker into her, perhaps to mimic Jesus' wounds on the cross.

On another occasion, Marcia recalled her mother rubbing hot chutney on her genitals on New Year's Eve when she was six or seven. The terrible part of this event, beyond being forced to lie naked on the kitchen floor and the pain of the hot sauce on her vulva and seeing her mother talking to herself and to some angel, was the recollection that her beloved father had come in, seen the event, and stormed off to bed. Any sense Marcia had had that her father didn't know about her mother's abuse of her vanished in the pain of such a recollection.

In yet another episode, after several weeks of severe upset, Marcia told me that there was blood on the walls. I inquired into it. It had been there intermittently for many years and always came up at times when she was convinced that her mother would do something terrible. The blood was associated with a feeling of impending terror, and often with her mother's voice threatening to "kill Jewish children". A number of sessions were spent on the hallucination of blood on the walls, with my repeatedly reality testing and asking if there was some meaning to this phenomenon. Slowly, in fits and starts of terror and abject cowering, Marcia told me about her mother's abortion. This happened when she was at home with her mother at the age of four; whether true or psychological truth I leave up to the reader.

Marcia's mother called her into the bathroom, screaming. There was blood and tissue everywhere; there was a knitting needle. Her mother yelled at her to clean up the blood. As she tried to clean it with a sponge, the blood smeared increasingly on the floor and walls of the bathroom. As she told me this, she was screaming that her mother had had an abortion; her mother told her that she had done this to kill her "Jewish baby". Marcia was crying and thrashing around on the floor as she related this. Suddenly she got up and started to run around the room, saying that there was meat burning. I replied that I couldn't smell anything. She insisted that something was burning, and then convulsively fell to the floor, sobbing and screaming that her mother had made her burn the baby. After a long period of talking about the sickly sweet smell of human flesh, she said that her mother, again talking to her angel, had said that this was a "Jewish baby" and needed to be incinerated. She had then made Marcia throw the remains of the foetus into the backyard incinerator.

At this point Marcia sobbed and sobbed, as I commiserated with her on what a terrible situation that would have been for a child, for there would have been not only the terror of the blood and the aborted foetus, but the mess of the blood on the walls, the hallucinating mother, and the sense that the child had done something terrible by putting the aborted foetus into the incinerator. I continued that the guilt belonged only to her mother and not to her, the child who had been forced to do these things. Sobbing became whimpering, florid emotion was replaced with calmness as Marcia gradually worked through this material.

Real? Not real? It seems hard to believe that Marcia's father could have just let a pregnancy go by without noticing its termination. Perhaps the mother said she had a miscarriage; perhaps the whole event was a psychological one. To me, unfortunately, it had the ring of truth. In any case, powerful affects and impressions were released, accepted and worked through in the course of our endeavour.

Other episodes were recollected both inside and outside the office. On one occasion, Marcia found herself increasingly distraught. Something was surfacing, but she didn't know what. After a Friday session she didn't go home, nor did she fragment and go to a bar or anywhere to meet someone. Instead, she found herself going to the woods of a state park, late in the day. As night fell, she lay on the ground in a secluded spot and covered herself with leaves and brush. She spent the night shivering and worrying about what would attack her. She went home in the morning, called me and told me what she had done. I asked if this had some meaning to her; she said no, not yet. By the time of her next session on Tuesday, she had recalled the episode of being buried in the hole in the back yard. In her own way, she had acted it out and than allowed it to surface into memory, with the usual diminution of internal chaos.

Sometimes I would get phone calls from "Margaret", an opinionated know-it-all, kind of like me, who had emerged during the course of treatment. "Margaret" would call in the following fashion: "Doctor, I thought you should know that Marcia isn't doing well this weekend, she's having a tough time" with whatever it happened to be. I would listen and tell my caller that it was really Marcia calling but she had fragmented herself due to some overwhelming issue that was coming up. "Margaret," I would continue, "you are just a better put-together aspect of Marcia; why don't you be really smart and realise that so that you can integrate yourself into Marcia and guide her through life's experiences? By the way, Margaret, you don't exist outside of Marcia." Margaret would say something to the effect of "if you say so, doctor".

I would often ask Marcia to look in the mirror when she was in a deluded altered state. Initially she would see the external confirmation of her internal belief, whether a four-year-old girl or a sixteen-year-old boy. Gradually, however, as our work proceeded (and with a slight amount of hectoring from me), her internal visual image of herself and her mirror image became more synchronous with who she was, a middle-aged woman.

The denouement of her self-fragmentation occurred more than ten years ago, when Marcia began to get upset again after a three-month calm and rational period. Sleep became more difficult, knives and ashes began to appear in her bedroom. All my statements that she must be doing it were met with her delusional certainty that her dead mother had returned to pursue her. Blood appeared on the walls again; her mother's voice was present, threatening all kinds of torture.

"Margaret" called to tell me that Marcia was decompensating. I asked to speak to Marcia, but the phone was hung up. Several hours later, between patients, there was a tray on my doorstep. On the tray were charred meat, ketchup (blood), burned cigarettes, gherkin pickles, a pile of ashes, a doll with its arms and legs torn off, and a butternut squash dressed as a little girl with a face painted on it and a knife stuck into the heart piercing a note saying "Die Jew" and signed with Marcia's mother's name.

I didn't know the precise significance to Marcia of all the objects on the tray, but it seemed ominous. I checked the surrounding area for her, was unable to find her, and called the police to put out an all points bulletin for her as a danger to herself. (I try to get automobile licence numbers for all of my most severely disturbed and potentially suicidal patients to thwart any suicidal acting out.) In addition, I alerted the toll plazas of the main bridges for a potential suicide.

I called Marcia a number of times over the next two hours, with no luck. Finally, just as I was about to call her family, she answered, seeming quite upset. She had just found herself in front of her house with ketchup all over her and wearing a red wig, the colour of her mother's hair. I explained to her over the phone what had just happened; she was in no condition to drive. This time, with the ketchup blood and the red wig, she was able to see that she had identified with her harsh and punishing mother and that some part of her was trying—in the guise of her mother—to harm herself. Marcia finally understood that it was she who was carrying on the patterns of her sadistic and psychotic mother towards herself. She seemed finally to realise that her mother was truly dead. Only she could harm herself.

During her session the next day Marcia reintegrated, and she has remained reintegrated for a number of years, as she has recognised that she was suffering from a delusional disorder of her sense of self in which she was the current perpetrator against herself of split off past abuses. The meaning of the tray, she told me, was as follows. The gherkins represented the digits of her fingers that her mother had threatened to cut off. The ketchup was blood; the charred meat represented the foetus which was burned. The doll that was torn asunder represented what would happen to Marcia if she told anyone about the tortures done to her. The burned cigarettes were to be used to burn her if she displeased her mother; the ashes were the remains of the cremated baby and what might become of her at her mother's hands. The squash doll with the knife and the message were self-explanatory.

For all practical purposes Marcia is healed and cured. She has gone into full-time work and has written a book on her life and treatment, as well as several other books. She has worked through a period of mourning for her lost delusional friends, her terror about being alone as one person, and her transference fear that her mother, being so evil, will somehow harm her from the grave. Marcia did remarkably well during the ten years I saw her, has given up all of her delusional presences, and is out of the woods. She has been without delusional presences for more than a decade. There may still be exacerbations and regressions, suicidal feelings, and a black emptiness inside. But if so, it is quite likely that all of these issues and feelings will be worked on in the usual therapeutic manner, as Marcia gradually works through the issues of her life. Little by little, intensive psychotherapy has changed what might be termed a trans-ference cure into lasting structural change.

Hopefully this case demonstrates that an intensive psychother-apy dealing with transference, resistance, unconscious motivation and dissociation, coupled with judicious reality testing, will allow even the most "untreatable" disturbed and delusional multiple personality to achieve psychic growth, healing, wellbeing and fusion into one being. From delusional certainty of a multiplicity of persons inhabiting one body, we achieve integration and psychological unity via interpretation. From her belief in many, Marcia has moved to recognition of her own frailty, vulnerability and feelings in the face of painful past circumstances and current apprehension. From her belief in many and her certainty that there was no consistency within or dependability without. Marcia has been re-parented during the course of an intensive psychotherapy and has identified with the therapeutic model internally, constantly monitoring herself. She now realises that she is only what we all are: one person with many aspects, hopefully integrated into one personality.

CHAPTER EIGHTEEN

The cheerleader

T ammy is a twenty-year-old woman who had a psychotic episode, partially related to psychedelic drug use. When I first saw her, she had been hospitalised for six and a half months, first in her home town for two months, then locally at the university hospital. After the transfer to San Francisco, she had regressed still further, requiring confinement to bed and forced feeding. After six and a half months in hospital, her diagnosis was acute and now chronic schizophrenia; psychedelic drug use was viewed as the factor that had tipped her over into psychosis. She came to my office for our first session obviously suffering severe muscular rigidity as a result of high antipsychotic drug use. This formerly pretty, vivacious cheerleader looked like a burnt out, dependent case.

Historically, Tammy was a bright first-year college student, a middle daughter living at home. She had lots of friends, loved to party, and did quite well at school. Her father was an aloof bureaucrat; her mother a very competent and concerned woman. Both parents valued the work ethic and were shocked that their daughters were so rebellious and (as it seemed to them) unmotivated.

During our first session, I asked Tammy what was bothering her. She responded that she was afraid of leaving the hospital. "Anything else?" I asked.

"Those voices are bothering me too."

"What do the voices say?" (She later told me that she had never been asked that question.)

Reluctantly, Tammy volunteered that she was pursued by voices in the shower telling her: "Bad people are going to kill me", and (sheepishly): "to shit in my father's mouth". Putting two and two together, I asked if she was angry about anything. Quickly, Tammy said: "Yes. I'm angry at being sent so far away from my boyfriend."

"I wonder if the voices might represent your anger at your parents, your father in particular—shitting in your father's mouth. Perhaps it has been hard for you to accept your anger as your own, so you've had voices, some of which are really your own feelings of anger, scaring you."

"I haven't thought about that," Tammy said reflectively and calmly.

By the next session (in three times per week outpatient therapy) the voices were gone. They did not return—if I am to believe her—during the remaining six months of Tammy's therapy with me. Then followed the process of weaning Tammy away from hospital, parents, medications, and me. She had been so frightened of the psychotic process and the voices that she had regressed. Now that she could begin to make sense of the voices, she wanted to become her old self as fast as possible; the regression was over.

I began to decrease Tammy's medicines gradually, as a result of both the side effects and her very favourable response to my comments about the meaning of her voices and how she had dealt with her anger by seeming to project it outside herself onto a voice. As the medicines diminished, she abruptly refused to take any antipsychotics.

Tammy raged about her parents sending her away, about the long hospitalisation, and at me for not authorising her immediate return home. I was concerned about her, since she was threatening to kill herself if I didn't send her home immediately. I saw her daily for four sessions, some of which were longer than normal, stayed in touch with the halfway house staff and Tammy during the evenings, and told the staff which bottle of cleanser to hide from her when she vociferously threatened to kill herself for three days.

It was a storm of emotion, which Tammy had kept walled up and controlled while in the hospital and heavily medicated. My goal was to help her integrate her feelings, not to bury them. This outpouring of energy and drama was interpreted to her as her difficulty tolerating her anger at the situation in general and me in particular for not acceding to her demands. She was expressing to me the fury she felt towards her parents. Within two weeks, as she accepted both realistic and transference aspects of her anger, her rage subsided.

Tammy continued therapy for five months, presenting now in her pre-morbid state, more of an impulsive adolescent. During the last months of therapy with me, her neediness, impulsivity and desire to regress from psychological conflict became the focus. Her anger at unmet needs became a central theme. She returned home in good shape, with no voices and off antipsychotic medication, ready to go back to cheerleading and college. There were two recommendations: to stay off drugs and to see a psychiatrist who understood the meaning of voices and delusions and was willing to work in a psychodynamic, exploratory fashion.

The obvious question is this. What would have happened had she seen someone who would try to understand her regression and voices in the first place? Would so much medicine and such a long hospitalisation have been necessary? I think not. From a hopeless, overly medicated, haggard, burnt out, hospitalised "untreatable" state, Tammy was quickly returned to her vivacious adolescent self, off antipsychotic medication, as the result of an intensive psychotherapy which made sense of previously terrifying hallucinations and a psychotic thought process. I can only ask how many other Tammys have been consigned to a life of long-term excessive antipsychotic medication when a little talking to the patient and attempting to make sense of hallucinations and delusions might have saved the day.

CHAPTER NINETEEN

Thoughts, lessons and conclusions

This book has hopefully highlighted some of the techniques and methods for using an intensive psychoanalytic psychotherapy in even the most disturbed and delusional patients. Even someone who was considered a hopelessly paranoid schizophrenic has responded to intensive psychotherapy, focusing on interpretations about and exploration of transference, psychotic thinking, and regressions to younger self states, supplemented by reality testing and confrontation of paranoid delusions. Severely delusional multiple personalities (patients with dissociative identity disorder), schizophrenic patients who had been delusional for decades, and delusional paranoid patients responded to this exploratory and potentially healing method.

I set out to demonstrate two principles which are linked together. The first is that in order to undermine, defuse and break into a delusional orientation, it is necessary to take a history of the origin and formation of the delusional system. The second and obvious result of the first process is the lessening of interest in (decathexis of) delusional reality and the upsurge of an interest in people and things and activities in the external world. It is my sense that a number of these cases have demonstrated the validity of both my approach and my hypotheses. The reader can best decide if this is the case.

I am left with a question. Since there is nothing new or startling about the approach I'm advocating, why did these patients not get appropriate treatment which offered the likelihood of change — even, in one case, after a decade at a famous long-term hospital? The answer, I'm afraid, is in the question. In the United States, at any rate, the field of psychiatry itself tends to abandon schizophrenics and delusional people, treating them (if at all) with reality testing, antipsychotic medication, socio-therapies and supportive psychotherapy, without dealing with the underlying thought disorder and its emotional and psychological origin.

The problem lies with us as psychiatrists and institutions. If the customary modalities of treatment do not work with delusional patients, we tend to give up on them or treat them in custodial fashion. We have been led to believe that an intensive psychotherapy will not work in the very disturbed schizophrenic or delusional patient, and hence do not try it when patients are unresponsive to the usual treatments. With many of these patients, everything had been tried already, with little effect. Unfortunately, no one had attempted to help them through the morass of paranoid and psychotic thinking by the one method that offered hope of a lasting change, perhaps cure: an intensive psychotherapy aimed at making clear to the patient the meaning of delusional thinking, misperceptions and hallucinations.

Even though these may sound like heroic psychotherapies, they were not. These cases illustrate the value of an uncovering psychotherapy that any patient with intelligence and means should expect, providing both a container and an explanation for previously chaotic and delusional productions, thinking and behaviour. It is clearly a good idea to embark on an interpretive psychodynamic psychotherapy of hallucinations and delusions sooner, rather than later. Patients need an understanding as to the possible meaning of these previously terrifying and disorganising phenomena. Right or wrong, exact or inexact, these attempts to make sense of voices, altered selves, delusions, paranoia and marked regression give the patient some structure from which to begin to view these hitherto fragmenting and destabilising phenomena.

Tammy responded positively during our first session; following which her hallucinations were gone. Lois, after seven years as a paranoid schizophrenic, rather quickly grasped the meaning of her delusions and cleared. Even Daphne, after 55 years of disturbance and ever so many hospitalisations, was able to make sense of her disorganisation and hallucinated realities, with the resultant amelioration of such an ominous and life-threatening picture. All of this happened through my use of an intensive psychotherapy of delusions, hallucinations, paranoia and altered self states. Why, then, is it so infrequently tried?

I am often asked how I work with such disturbed patients. How do I have the arrogance or perseverance to believe I can prevail with such disturbed and delusional patients? My response is that I am lucky enough to have found in my earliest dealings with psychotic patients during medical school that their behaviour made sense to me and, with work, to them. Later, while working with Ronnie Laing, David Cooper and Aaron Esterson at Villa 21 at Shenley Hospital, near London, in the mid 1960s, I found colleagues who had a similar view that there was meaning in delusional hospitalised patients' thoughts and behaviour. Here, the focus was on an existential understanding of psychosis. In my psychiatric residency and in practice, as this book has hopefully demonstrated, I elaborated on this conviction that delusional and psychotic behaviour not only had unconscious meaning to the patient but could be made understandable to the patient in the form of a healing exploratory dynamic psychotherapy, in conjunction with antipsychotic medication used in a judicious fashion.

I am also often asked how I have the tolerance to deal with such intrapsychic pain and disorganisation, and how I tolerate the feelings, fantasies, delusions and memories that repeatedly come up. My answer is both simple and complicated. I have the conviction that a psychodynamic psychotherapy, with appropriate and judicious use of whatever medications are required, has a very good chance of aiding the patient in understanding him or herself and starting the process of emotional growth and change. This process is short for some, many years for others. With such a belief, buttressed by numerous clinical examples, I am able to "weather the storms" and any sense of discouragement or questions about the slowness of change. Over the years, my commitment to, and tenacity in, working with such delusional patients rather than frightening them away has been amply rewarded by the clinical gains of patients and the positive reactions of my colleagues. Both have made me feel even more confident of the potential benefits of such a psychotherapeutic approach.

It is, of course, very important to ask oneself, if there is only slow or halting progress, what types of resistance to change might be occurring. Could the patient still have other delusions? Could there be some unexamined transference or countertransference issue, for example too much control of the patient, or infantilisation, or too little empathy perceived? Do medications need modification? Invariably, one must look at these possible questions and paradigms and sort them through.

As to the question about tolerating the intensity of affect and recollection that occurs with such patients, I believe it is quintessential to be present to the pain of another, as well as present to my own empathic reverberations and registration of this pain. Allowing feelings and fantasies to "play through" in a relatively non-attached (although not detached) fashion has enabled me to both tolerate external and internal pain and observe the interpersonal and transferential situation at the same time. Of course, some patients sensing this central core of calmness in me become infuriated, since they possess nothing like it, and try to up the ante with various verbal and occasionally physical attacks. Perhaps they resent it; perhaps there is a transference issue of neglect from the parents and a misinterpretation of my response to them. With the work of therapy, however, these issues may be worked through in the usual "grist for the mill" fashion.

In addition, as advice for any who may want to pursue such work, I have many other interests that sustain me and nurture my generally optimistic attitude to life. As far as I am concerned, it is imperative to have time and passionate involvement in areas unrelated to working with delusional patients, in order to be able to work with such disturbed people without succumbing to despair in the face of such pain and chaos.

I'm sure I have made many mistakes—of omission, commission, technique or theory—in working with these patients. The important thing to keep in mind in working with delusional patients is that a mistake is hardly ever an all or nothing event. If your heart and interest are with the patient, he or she will sense it and any mistakes can be discussed in the usual psychotherapeutic working through of material. If it becomes an extreme, all or nothing event, this says something about the patient and his or her dynamics.

Working with such delusional and disturbed patients is not an eight hours a day job. People know they can call me at my home office if it's urgent. I'd rather talk to someone who is decompensating for a few minutes, helping them understand the situation or suggesting some medication if necessary, rather than have them totally fall apart. It seems the better part of discretion to maintain close contact with patients going through great difficulties. At times, I bring my work home with me, thinking about what else might be done to help ensure the safety that night of someone going through a difficult time, such as giving up a delusion or a whole delusional system. This is a time of great vulnerability, for the delusion serves a defensive function: it serves to keep someone from both pain and life's experiences. Sometimes I'll give a patient who is going through a great deal of difficulty a call or two in the evening or at the weekend, to let them know they're not alone and to give whatever succour is required. At other times, I might have a dream, which is often illuminating about transference or countertransference issues with patients. I usually bring the dream up, both because patients like the fact that I care enough about them to dream about them and our relationship, and because the issues and conclusions presented in the dreams are often so pertinent to whatever clinical dilemma may be occurring.

Exploration and interpretation of intrapsychic conflict, resistance, transference and countertransference are some of the major tools that psychodynamic psychotherapists possess. Yet we often eschew our psychoanalytic orientation towards the full understanding of our patients when confronted with schizophrenia and delusional states. I hope this book has clearly made the point that an uncovering exploratory dynamic psychotherapy can aid in the recovery, healing and cure of even the most disturbed schizophrenic and delusional patients across a number of different diagnostic categories. Since healing and cures are possible through such an intensive psychotherapy, why is this form of psychotherapy so infrequently practised, in conjunction with the judicious use of medications?

My only conclusion is that we, as a field, have lost our way in treating severely disturbed and delusional patients. Dealing with insurance companies, threading our way through the latest pharmaceutical claims and the incessant advertising of drug companies trying to increase their sales, listening to teachers who have not been successful with the intensive psychotherapy of schizophrenia, following psychiatric department chairmen who emphasise the "scientific" approach, as the generation of the psychoanalytic department chairman has given way to the generation of the biochemist and molecular biologist, reading journals biased towards the biological, the field of psychiatry has concluded that the intensive psychotherapy of schizophrenia cannot be done.

Antipsychotic medications help many patients. If so, fine; then our task is easier. But if delusions and schizophrenic thinking and hallucinations persist, an attempt should be made to help the patient understand the psychological underpinnings of his or her delusions. Once understood through an exploratory psychotherapy of the whole person, delusions and schizophrenic thinking included, an attempt may be made to diminish antipsychotics. As some of these cases demonstrate, delusional patients may have medications titrated down and stopped, as an understanding of delusional thought and psychotic thinking and behaviour take hold.

As a field, we have adopted a cult-like attitude to the alleged benefits of antipsychotic drugs and supportive psychotherapy (Deikman, 1990). This is not to throw out the baby with the bathwater. I certainly use antipsychotic medication. However, these medications may have serious side effects in a large number of patients, and often don't do the job for which they're prescribed. All too often, psychiatrists and hospitals use medication as the main treatment, never bothering to ferret out and attempt to help the psychotic patient understand what is going on psychologically and symbolically. When questioned about such an approach, many treating psychiatrists say that the psychotic patient is incapable of making progress and that antipsychotic medication is the best that can be done. They are wrong, as I hope these cases have demonstrated. I use these medications in conjunction with an intensive dynamic psychotherapy aimed at helping the deeply disturbed patient understand his delusions, hallucinations and schizophrenic thoughts. I recommend such an approach to other therapists.

As psychiatrists and psychotherapists, we do not pay enough attention to studies which show that antipsychotics and supportive ancillary therapies may lead to patients with less motivation and initiative, and poorer prognosis than those treated prior to the general use of antipsychotics (Bockoven & Solomon, 1975), nor to studies in twenty-year follow-up, before antipsychotics, demonstrating that

"60-85% of schizophrenic patients, depending on the criteria used, had achieved good social recovery" (Mosher, 1987). The recent study showing that a high percentage of patients off antipsychotics had better global functioning than those on antipsychotics (Harrow & Jobe, 2007) will most probably meet a similar fate.

Many practitioners (Rosenfeld, 1965; Boyer & Giovacchini, 1967; Guntrip, 1968; Fromm-Reichmann, 1950; Will, 1968; Sechehaye, 1951; Lidz, 1973; Pao, 1979; Giovacchini, 1979) have written about the benefits of intensive psychotherapy leading to intrapsychic change and healing in schizophrenia, but most of the profession has gone in a different direction. My colleagues at ISPS, the International Society for the Psychological Treatments of the Schizophrenias and Other Psychoses, provide a sympathetic, warm and stimulating counter-balance to the prevailing trends in the usual treatments of schizo-phrenia and delusional disorders.

I hope some of you, after reading this book, will reconsider your positions about the primacy of antipsychotics, supportive psycho-therapy and ancillary therapies in the treatment of delusional dis-orders such as schizophrenia, paranoia, and multiple personality (dissociative identity) disorder. I hope some of you will begin to follow your analytic understanding of a patient's pathology into an intensive psychotherapy which offers the patient the best chance of intrapsychic integration of even the most delusional thinking and behaviour.

The cases presented in this book speak for themselves. Using an intensive psychodynamic psychotherapy, in conjunction with judicious antipsychotic drug use, these previously hopeless and "untreatable" schizophrenic and delusional patients have been given the opportunity for recovery, healing and cure, where the best previ-ously achieved with a supportive approach and antipsychotics was a chronic delusional orientation and disintegration. Using an intensive psychotherapy of schizophrenia and delusional states, some of these "untreatable" psychotic patients improved, some recovered, some healed and some were cured. To my mind, the choice of therapeutic method is clear.

Long-term studies on schizophrenia

Brian Koehler, PhD
(*From the ISPS-US website*)

I thought it would be helpful to summarise the actual data on long-term follow-up studies in schizophrenia since there are still so many myths surrounding this area. I am still amazed to hear graduate students in various mental health disciplines speak of the "incurability" of severe mental illness. I derived the following information primarily from "Beyond dementia praecox: findings from long-term follow-up studies of schizophrenia" by Joseph Calabrese and Patrick Corrigan (2004).

The Burghölzli hospital study (Switzerland)

Manfred Bleuler (son of Eugen Bleuler, who was director of the Burghölzli clinic in Zurich and gave us the name "schizophrenia") followed a cohort of 208 patients for an average of 23 years. This cohort included both first admissions and readmissions to the hospital during 1942 and 1943. The diagnostic criteria emphasised psychotic symptomatology. The results indicated that 53% of the group participants overall and 66% of the first admission participants were judged to have recovered or be significantly improved. Fully recovered participants comprised 23% of the first admission group and 20% of all research participants.

The Iowa 500 study (United States)

In the Iowa 500 study, 186 persons with schizophrenia were followed for an average of 35 years. The researchers also included a group with affective disorder and a control group of 160 surgical patients. Compared to people from the other psychiatric groups (i.e. with a diagnosis of affective or schizoaffective disorder), 46% of those people with schizophrenia had improved or recovered.

The Bonn hospital study (Germany)

This study followed 502 persons with schizophrenia for an average of 22.4 years. The results were that 22% of the research participants had complete remission of symptoms, 43% had non-characteristic types of remission (defined as involving non-psychotic symptomatology such as cognitive disturbances, lack of energy, sleep disturbances and hypersensitivity; in regard to the last of these, some patients have described this state as a type of "skinlessness"), and 35% experienced characteristic schizophrenia residual syndromes. Therefore, 65% had a more favourable outcome than would have been expected from clinical experience. In regard to social functioning, 56% of all participants were judged to be "fully recovered", which was defined in this study as full-time employment. At the last follow-up, 13.3% were permanently hospitalised.

The Lausanne study (Switzerland)

This study reported the longest follow-up of the major long-term studies. The researchers, who included Luc Ciompi, followed 289 participants for an average of 37 years and up to a total of 64 years. The results indicated that 27% reached a stabilised 5-year end state of recovery, 22% reached an end state described as "mild", 24% were described as "moderately severe", and 18% were judged to have a "severe" end state. There was a 14% rate of continuous hospitalisation.

The Chestnut Lodge Hospital (United States)

In this study, 446 (72%) of the persons treated between 1950 and 1975 at Chestnut Lodge Psychiatric Hospital in Rockville, Maryland were followed for an average of 15 years. This site specialised in psychoanalytically-oriented long-term residential treatment. The research population consisted of persons with chronic and treatment-resistan mental illness. The researchers used a highly restrictive definition of recovery: full-time employment, absence of symptomatology and need for treatment, meaningful engagement in family and social activities. The results were that two thirds (64%) of the persons with schizophrenia were judged to be chronically ill or marginally functional. One third (36%) were recovered or functioning adequately. The investigators reported that the recoveries included persons who had been viewed as hopeless chronic cases.

The Japanese long-term study

This study took place at Gumma University Hospital in Japan. One hundred and five persons with schizophrenia discharged between 1958 and 1962 were followed for a period of 21 to 27 years. Thirty-one percent of the participants were judged to be recovered, 46% improved, and 23% unimproved. Results on social outcome indicated that 47% were fully or partially self-supportive and 31% were hospitalised.

The Vermont longitudinal research project (United States)

This study, conducted by ISPS member Courtney Harding and colleagues, followed 269 persons for an average of 32 years. The participants had been ill for an average of 16 years and were hospitalised on the back wards of Vermont State Hospital for six years. This study is unique in that the participants were involved in an innovative rehabilitation programme and were released with community support already in place. DSM-III criteria were used. At follow-up, one half to two thirds of all participants were considered to have improved or recovered. Of the living participants with schizophrenia, 68% did not display further symptoms or signs of schizophrenia at follow-up. Almost half (45%) of the participants displayed no psychiatric symptoms at all. More than two thirds (68%) of the participants were assessed as having good functioning on the Global Assessment Scale, which provides a global measure of social and psychological functioning.

The Maine-Vermont comparison study (United States)

This study compared the outcomes of 269 persons with schizophrenia in Maine with the outcomes of the 269 persons in the Vermont longitudinal study. The average follow-up period for the Maine participants was 36 years and 32 years for the Vermont participants. The persons in the Vermont study were exposed to a model rehabilitative programme organised around the goal of self-sufficiency, immediate residential and vocational placements in the community, and long-term continuity of care. The Maine participants received standard psychiatric care. Results of this study showed that the Vermont participants at follow-up were more productive, and had fewer symptoms, better community adjustment and better global functioning than the Maine participants. Approximately one half (49%) of the Maine participants were rated as having good functioning on the Global Assessment Scale, the primary global measure used for both Maine and Vermont participants. The authors suggested that it was the provision of the model rehabilitative programme which accounted for the difference between the groups.

The Cologne long-term study (Germany)

This study followed 148 persons with a DSM-III diagnosis of schizophrenia and 101 persons with schizoaffective disorder for an average of 25 years. The results showed that 6.8% of persons with schizophrenia had full psychopathological remission and 51.4% had non-characteristic residua. Therefore, 58.2% had a more favourable outcome than would have been expected with schizophrenia.

The World Health Organisation international study of schizophrenia

The WHO Study of Schizophrenia is a long-term follow-up study of 14 culturally diverse, treated incidence cohorts and four prevalence cohorts comprising 1,633 persons diagnosed with schizophrenia and other psychotic illnesses. Global outcomes at 15 and 25 years were assessed to be favourable for more than 50% of all participants. The researchers observed that 56% of the incidence cohort and 60% of the prevalence cohort were judged to be recovered. Those participants with a specific diagnosis of schizophrenia had a recovery rate which was close to 50%. Geographic factors were significant in terms of both symptoms and social disability. Certain research locations were associated with a greater chance of recovery even in those participants with unfavourable early-onset illness courses. The course and outcome for persons diagnosed with schizophrenia were far better in the "developing countries" than in the "developed" world of Western Europe and America.

The first of the WHO studies, the International Pilot Study of Schizophrenia (IPSS), assessed 1,202 persons diagnosed with schizophrenia in nine countries. The results showed that persons with schizophrenia in the "developing" world (e.g. Colombia, India and Nigeria) had better outcomes than persons in the "developed" countries (e.g. Moscow, London, Washington, Prague, Aarhus [Denmark]). Overall, 52% of persons in the developing countries were assessed to be in the "best" category of outcome (defined in this study as an initial episode only, followed by full or partial recovery) compared with 39% in the developed countries. This finding was also reported in a five-year follow-up research study. In this study, 73% of those participants from the developing world were in the best outcome group compared with 52% in the developed world. A second study, called the Determinants of Outcome of Severe Mental Disorder (DOSMD), used more rigorous criteria and followed more than 1,300 patients in 10 countries and, like the IPSS, discovered that the highest rates of recovery occurred in the developing world. At a two-year follow-up, 56% of those in the developing world were in the best outcome group compared to 39% of the participants from the developed countries. The finding of better outcome for persons in the developing countries applied whether the illness was acute or gradual in onset, and has been attributed to factors such as family environment and expressed emotion, social role expectations, stigma and discrimination, etc.

These findings by the WHO have been criticised on the basis of differences in follow-up, arbitrary grouping of centres into developed or developing, diagnostic ambiguities (e.g. narrow versus broad definition of schizophrenia), selective outcome measures, gender-related factors, as well as age. However, a recent reanalysis of the data by Hopper and Wanderling (2000) demonstrates convincingly that not a single one of these criticisms is sufficient to explain away the findings of differential course and outcome in schizophrenia favouring persons in the developing countries. These are surprisingly robust findings.

Harding, Zubin and Strauss (1987) noted that the development of chronic illness in persons with schizophrenia "may be viewed as having less to do with any inherent natural outcome of the disorder and more to do with a myriad of environmental and other psychosocial factors interacting with the person and the illness" (p. 483). In regard to all of the follow-up studies, Calabrese and Corrigan (2004) concluded:

> Each of these studies found that rather than having a progressively deteriorating course, schizophrenia has a heterogeneous range of courses from severe cases requiring repeated or continuous hospitalisation to cases in which a single illness episode is followed by complete remission of symptoms. The findings reported in these studies as a whole indicate that roughly half of the participants recovered or significantly improved over the long term, suggesting that remission or recovery is much more common than originally thought. [p. 71]

The role of medication

Most clinicians would agree that judicious use of medications, including antipsychotic agents, plays a significant role in the treatment of acute psychotic disturbance. However, in the question of maintenance treatment it proves to be more difficult to ascertain valid guidelines for many patients. Manfred Bleuler (1974) noted that of all his patients who maintained long-standing remissions or a stable recovery, not a single one had been on chronic neuroleptic medication. Instead, the patients were given medication during acute phases and never for longer than a few weeks after they had recovered from their acute episode. Harding and Zahniser (1994), in their assessment of the long-term follow-up literature, observed that at least 25% to 50% of participants were completely off medications, experienced no further symptoms of schizophrenia, and were functioning well.

We need to know a great deal more about the relationship between symptomatology, subjective suffering, cultural-environmental factors which are demonstrated to be neuroprotective or neurodisorganising, and gene expression and neurochemistry in general and within each individual patient, before we can validly assert the need for continued long-term use of antipsychotic medications. Most patients are prescribed medications without corroborating studies of saturation levels in different receptor systems (such as can be done in research studies with PET or MRS but is not practical for everyday clinical settings) in neural pathways of import—for we know that there is not always an isomorphic relationship between neurotransmitter and neuromodulator levels and clinical symptomatology, e.g. serotonin levels and levels of depression. Symptoms such as delusions and hallucinations, as clinicians are well aware, do not always (or perhaps even often) respond to changing neurochemistry in the theoretically desired direction. The human brain is so incredibly complex: in addition to the dozens of identified neurotransmitters, there are over 60 identified neuropeptides, many of which, such as the neurokinins (substance P, neurokinin A and B) and neurotensin (coexists with dopamine and modulates dopamine-induced behaviours), have been suggested to play a role in psychosis. We must all remain humble as to the big questions regarding psychosis therapy and in understanding the biological aetiology and correlates of this group of disorders. However, despite our ignorance, many patients are able to recover significantly (or get better than they had been prior to the index episode) on their own or with the support of significant others and the myriad of treatments we have at our disposal to assist persons in their recovery process.

In regard to the above data, I ask myself: what kind of neurological illness or group of illnesses is schizophrenia? These disorders do not behave like traditional neurodegenerative disorders in which there is no significant degree of recovery or full remission (some of which are seen in advanced age and cannot be fully attributed to a "burnout" process, since the Maine-Vermont Comparison Study demonstrated the importance for the Vermont participants of psychosocial interventions). The neuroscience research findings in schizophrenia are largely non-specific and overlap with the neuroscience findings in profound and chronic stress, fear, anxiety and social isolation. I believe that what we call schizophrenia is a disorder of the self, and the self emerges biologically, intersubjectively and culturally within particular contexts. All of these levels are coactive, with significant feed-forward and feedback processes operating in non-linear modes and interdigitated with random as well as subjective (agency, will, autonomy) processes.

Brief review of the history of psychoanalytic perspectives on schizophrenia

Brian Koehler, PhD
(From the ISPS-US website)

F reud believed that the illness he named as one of the narcissistic neuroses, schizophrenia, is triggered by a withdrawal of
emotional investment in external or internal objects secondary to what we would today call a narcissistic injury. In his view,
positive symptoms such as hallucinations and delusions were restitutive, i.e. attempts at self-cure. Freud saw the core problem as
a decathexis of objects (a "silent lesion" if you will—perhaps the
psychoanalytic analogue of the "silent genetic or prenatal lesion"
identified in current neurodevelopmental theories—which inter-
acts with later normal brain development to bring about the clinical
picture of psychosis) and a hypercathexis of the ego (which is how
he explained such phenomena as grandiosity and hypochondriasis).
Freud's famous comment that a delusion is like a patch applied over
the tear between the ego and the external world reflects on his viewpoint of symptoms as restitutive, i.e. an attempt to reforge object ties.
Freud saw the central conflict as one between the id and the external

world in which the latter becomes remodelled to fit the needs of the beleaguered patient. Federn understood schizophrenia to be a problem of too little narcissistic investment in one's ego boundaries. Edith Jacobson emphasised the lack of differentiation between self and other. Jung emphasised the importance of the feeling-toned pathogenic complexes and the role of trauma in schizophrenia.

Sullivan understood schizophrenia to be the result of severe and dissociative warping of the personality and self-esteem. Sullivan, like Melanie Klein, emphasised the role of severe anxiety (what Marvin Hurvich would refer to as annihilation anxiety) and loneliness. Frieda Fromm-Reichmann stressed the strong conflicts between dependency and hostility. Melanie Klein emphasised the role of projective identification, schizoid anxiety (a feeling of falling into bits—unintegration) and the predominance of paranoid-schizoid narcissistic functioning over more integrated depressive anxieties and guilt.

Bion emphasised that we all have psychotic and non-psychotic parts of our personalities. He saw the psychotic person to be under the sway of terror: a fear of being eaten up not just by the therapist or the hospital, but by her- or himself as well. Bion speculated that the patient is painfully aware of being dependent upon someone outside the self and being all alone at the same time. Hanna Segal (personal communication) believed that her most significant contribution to psychoanalysis was her concept of the symbolic equation, in which symbol and symbolised become equivalent in the psychotic patient's mind. Herbert Rosenfeld emphasised that the psychotic person projects so much of her- or himself into the other that there is a paranoid reaction of being colonised and invaded because of pathological projective identification. Winnicott noted that what we see clinically in psychosis is a defence structure developed around unthinkable, primitive agonies. (Winnicott thought that anxiety was too mild a word for this state.)

Elvin Semrad and David Garfield saw schizophrenia to be the result of ego breakdown triggered by unbearable anxiety and other affects. Harold Searles emphasised both conflict and deficit and the importance of one's countertransference in helping the patient to reconstitute a firmer sense of self and identity. Ping-Nie Pao, like Margaret Mahler, understood schizophrenia to be reflective of a derailment in separation-individuation with symbiotic deficits. Pao thought that as a result of conflict over separation, sex and aggression, the person experiences organismic panic and a paralysis of integrative ego function, with a pathological reorganisation of self which is evident in grandiose and persecutory delusions.

Kohut emphasised building an empathic bridge to shore up a non-cohesive and fragmented self. Parenthetically, towards the end of his life, Kohut reversed his position that psychoanalysis could not be used with persons with schizophrenia, and he reported treating patients with paranoid delusions. He saw the latter as a psychologically meaningful way of expressing emotional states.

Lacan viewed schizophrenia as a foreclosure of the key signifier "name-of-the-father." The latter helps the developing child move beyond imaginary and symbiotic entanglements with the primary caregiver. Bert Karon underscores the sense of terror in psychosis and Ann-Louise Silver and Stefanie Glennon emphasise authentic interpersonal engagement. Gaetano Benedetti and Maurizio Peciccia understand the danger in schizophrenia to always be one of self-loss, and this can occur at the poles of autonomy or relatedness. They see the structural problem in schizophrenia to be a de-integration of the separate and symbiotic selves. These are a few of the contributions psychoanalysts have made to the field of psychosis psychotherapy. I have, regretfully, left out many of the contributions which friends and colleagues of mine in ISPS (www.isps.org and www.isps-us.org) have made.

REFERENCES

Ackerman, N. W. (1958). *The Psychodynamics of Family Life*. New York: Basic Books.

Arlow, J. & Brenner, C. (1964). *Psychoanalytic Concepts and the Structural Theory*. New York: International Universities Press.

Bion, W. R. (1962). A Theory of Thinking. In: *Second Thoughts*. London: Heinemann.

Bleuler, M. (1974). The long-term course of the schizophrenic psychoses. *Psychological Medicine, 4*: 244–254.

Bliss, E. L. & Jeppsen, E. A. (1985). Prevalence of Multiple Personality among Inpatients and Outpatients. *Amer. Jnl. Psychiatry, 142*: 250–251.

Bliss, E. L. & Larson, E. M. (1985). Sexual criminality and hypnotisability. *Journal of Nervous and Mental Disease, 173*: 522–526.

Bockoven, J. S. & Solomon, L. C. (1975). Comparison of two five-year follow-up studies: 1947–1952 and 1967–1972. *Am. J. Psychiatry, 132*: 796–801.

Boyer, L. B. & Giovacchini, P. L. (1967). *Psychoanalytic Treatment of Schizophrenic and Characterological Disorders*. New York: Science House.

Boyer, L. B. (1971). Psychoanalytic Technique in the Treatment of Certain Characterological and Schizophrenic Disorders. *Int. J. Psychoanal. 52*: 67–85.

Boyer, L. B. (1983). *The Regressed Patient*. New York: Jason Aronson.

Calabrese, J. D. & Corrigan, P. W. (2004). Beyond dementia praecox: findings from long-term follow-up studies of schizophrenia. In: Ruth O. Ralph & Patrick W. Corrigan (Eds.), *Recovery in Mental Illness: Broadening Our Understanding of Wellness*. Washington DC: American Psychological Association.

Cameron, M. (1995). *Broken Child*. New York: Kensington.

Carpenter, W. T., Strauss, J. S. & Bartko, J. J. (1973). Flexible System for the Diagnosis of Schizophrenia: Report from the WHO International Pilot Study of Schizophrenia. *Science, 182*: 1257–1278.

Crane, G. E. (1973). Persistent Dyskinesia. *Br. J. Psychiatry, 122*: 395–405.

Deikman, A. J. & Whitaker, L. C. (1979). Humanizing a Psychiatric Ward: Changing from Drugs to Psychotherapy. *Psychotherapy: Theory, Research & Practice, 16*: 204–214.

Deikman, A. J. (1990). *The Wrong Way Home: Uncovering the Patterns of Cult Behavior in American Society*. Boston: Beacon.

Ellenberger, H. F. (1970). *The Discovery of the Unconscious: The History and Evolution of Dynamic Psychiatry*. New York: Basic Books.

Fleck, S. (1985). Review of Stone, 1983 (see below). *Psychoanalytic Quarterly 54*: 299–305.

Freud, S. & Breuer, J. (1893). On the Psychical Mechanism of Hysterical Phenomena Collected Papers. Vol 1. London, International Psychoanalytic Press.

Freud, S. (1894). Neuro-Psychoses of Defence. *SE 3*.

Freud, S. & Breuer, J. (1895). Studies on Hysteria. *SE 2*.

Freud, S. (1896). The Aetiology of Hysteria. *SE 3*.

Freud, S. (1911). Psychoanalytic Notes on an Autobiographical Account of a Case of Paranoia. *SE 12*.

Freud, S. (1915). The Unconscious. *SE 14*.

Fromm-Reichmann, F. (1950). *Principles of Intensive Psychotherapy*. Chicago: University of Chicago Press.

Fromm-Reichmann, F. (1959). *Psychoanalysis and Psychotherapy: Selected Papers*. Chicago: University of Chicago Press.

Giovacchini, P. L. (1979). *Treatment of Primitive Mental States*. New York: Jason Aronson.

Grinspoon, L., Ewalt, J. R. & Shader, R. I. (1967). Long-term Treatment of Chronic Schizophrenia. *Int. J. Psychiatry, 4*: 116–128.

Grotstein, J. (1981). *Splitting and Projective Identification*. New York: Jason Aronson.

Gunderson, J. G. & Mosher, L. R. (1975). *Psychotherapy of Schizophrenia*. New York: Jason Aronson.

Gunderson, J. G., Frank, A. F., Katz, H. N., Vannicelli, M. L., Frosch, J. P.

& Knapp, P. H. (1984).Effects of Psychotherapy in Schizophrenia. II: Comparative Outcome of Two Forms of Treatment. *Schiz. Bull. 10*: 564–598.

Guntrip, H. (1961). *Personality Structure and Human Interaction*. London: Hogarth.

Guntrip, H. (1968). *Schizoid Phenomena, Object Relations and the Self*. London: Hogarth Press and Institute of Psycho-Analysis.

Harding, C. M., Zubin, J. & Strauss, J. S. (1987). Chronicity in Schizophrenia: Fact, Partial Fact, or Artifact? *Hospital and Community Psychiatry, 38*: 477–486.

Harding, C. M. & Zahniser, J. H. (1994). Empirical Correction of Seven Myths about Schizophrenia with Implications for Treatment. *Acta Psychiatrica Scandinavica, 90 (Suppl. 384)*: 140–146.

Harrow, M. & Jobe, T. H. (2007). Factors Involved in Outcome and Recovery in Schizophrenia Patients not on Antipsychotic Medications: a 15-year Multifollow-up Study. *Journal of Nervous and Mental Disease, 195*: 406–414.

Hopper, K. & Wanderling, J. (2000). Revisiting the Developed vs. Developing Country Distinction in Course and Outcome in Schizophrenia: Results from ISoS, the WHO-Collaborative Follow-up Project. *Schiz. Bull. 26*: 835–846.

Jackson, M. & Williams, P. (1994). *Unimaginable Storms: A Search for Meaning in Psychosis*. London: Karnac.

Jackson, M. (2001). *Weathering the Storms: Psychotherapy for Psychosis*. London: Karnac.

Jones, M. (1953). *The Therapeutic Community*. New York: Basic Books.

Jung, C. G. (1960). *The Psychogenesis of Mental Disease*. London: Routledge.

Karon, B. P. & Vandenbos, G. R. (1981). *Psychotherapy of Schizophrenia: The Treatment of Choice*. New York: Jason Aronson.

Karon, B. P. (1984). The Fear of Reducing Medications, and Where Have all the Patients Gone? *Schiz. Bull. 10*: 613–617.

Klerman, G. L. (1984). Ideology and Science in the Individual Psychotherapy of Schizophrenia. *Schiz. Bull. 10*: 608–612.

Klein, D. F., Gittleman, R., Quitkin, F. & Rifkin, A. (1980). *Diagnosis and Drug Treatment of Psychiatric Disorders: Adults and Children*. Baltimore: Williams & Wilkins.

Klein, M. (1948). *Contributions to Psychoanalysis, 1921–1945*. London: Hogarth.

Kluft, R. P. (1984). Treatment of Multiple Personality Disorder: a Study of 33 Cases. *Psychiatric Clin. North Amer, 7*: 9–29.

Kohut, H. (1977). *The Restoration of the Self.* New York: Int. Univ. Press.

Laing, R. D. (1960). *The Divided Self: An Existential Study in Sanity and Madness.* London: Penguin.

Laing, R. D. (1961). *The Self and Others: Further Studies in Sanity and Madness.* London: Penguin.

Laing, R. D. (1976). *The Facts of Life.* London: Penguin.

Lidz, T. (1973). *Origin and Treatment of Schizophrenic Disorders.* New York: Basic Books.

Masson, J. M. (1984). *The Assault on Truth: Freud's Suppression of the Seduction Theory.* New York: Farrar, Straus & Giroux.

May, P. A. (1968). *Treatment of Schizophrenia: A Comparative Study of Five Treatment Methods.* New York: Science House.

Mosher, L. R. (1987). Review of *Recovery From Schizophrenia: Psychiatry and Political Economy* by Richard Warner. *Am. J. Psychiatry, 144:* 956–957.

Ogden, T. (1989). *The Primitive Edge of Experience.* London: Karnac.

Orne, M. (1989). Psych News, Dec. 1, p. 2.

Pao, P. N. (1979). *Schizophrenic Disorders: Theory and Treatment from a Psychodynamic Point of View.* New York: International Universities Press.

Putnam, F. W. (1989). *Diagnosis and Treatment of Multiple Personality Disorder.* New York: Guilford.

Putnam, F. W., Guroff, J. J., Silberman, E. K., Barban, L. & Post, R. M. (1986). The Clinical Phenomenology of Multiple Personality Disorder: a Review of 100 Recent Cases. *Journal of Clinical Psychiatry, 47:* 285–293.

Putnam, F. W. (1986a). Scientific Investigation of Multiple Personality Disorder. In: J. M. Quen (Ed.), *Split Minds/Split Brains.* New York: New York University Press.

Putnam, F. W. (1986b). The Treatment of Multiple Personality: State of the Art. In: B. G. Braun (Ed.), *The Treatment of Multiple Personality Disorder* (pp. 175–198). Washington DC: American Psychiatric Press.

Rosen, J. (1962). *Direct Psychoanalytic Psychiatry.* New York: Grune & Stratton.

Rosenbaum, M. (1980). The Role of the Term Schizophrenia in the Decline of Diagnoses of Multiple Personality. *Arch. Gen. Psychiatry, 37:* 1383–1385.

Rosenfeld, H. A. (1965). *Psychotic States.* London: Hogarth.

Schlesinger, H. J. (1969). Diagnosis and Prescription for Psychotherapy. *Bull. Menninger Clinic 33:* 269–278.

Schreiber, F. R. (1974). *Sybil.* London: Penguin.

Searles, H. (1965). *Collected Papers on Schizophrenia and Related Subjects.* London: Hogarth.

Searles, H. (1975). Countertransference and Theoretical Model. In: J. G. Gunderson & L. R. Mosher (Eds.), *Psychotherapy of Schizophrenia* (pp. 223–228). New York: Jason Aronson.

Sechehaye, M. A. (1951). *Symbolic Realization: A New Method of Psychotherapy Applied to a Case of Schizophrenia.* New York, International Universities Press.

Smith, D. B. (2007). *Muses, Madmen, and Prophets: Hearing Voices and the Borders of Sanity.* London: Penguin.

Stanton, A. H., Gunderson, J.G., Frank, A.F., Vannicelli, M. L., Schnitzer, R. & Rosenthal, R. (1984). Effects of Psychotherapy in Schizophrenia. I: Design and Implementation of a Controlled Study. *Schiz. Bull. 10*: 520–563.

Stone, M. H., Albert, H. D., Forrest, D. V. & Arieti, S. (1983). *Treating Schizophrenic Patients. A Clinico-Analytical Approach.* New York: McGraw Hill.

Sullivan, H. S. (1962). *Schizophrenia as a Human Process.* New York: Norton.

Van der Kolk, B. & Van der Hart, O. (1989). Pierre Janet and the Breakdown of Adaptation in Psychological Trauma. *American Journal of Psychiatry, 146*: 1530–1540.

Vaughan, S. C. (1997). *The Talking Cure: The Science Behind Psychotherapy.* New York: Putnam's.

Wexler, M. (1971). Schizophrenia as conflict and deficiency. *Psychoanalytic Quarterly, 40*: 83–100.

Will, O. A. (1968). Schizophrenia and Psychotherapy. In: J. Marmor (Ed.), *Modern Psychoanalysis.* New York: Basic Books.

Winniciott, D. W. (1958). *Collected Papers: Through Paediatrics to Psychoanalysis.* London: Tavistock.